PostGame Pass

PostGame Pass

ACCESS INTO "THE LIFE"

Jill Munroe

ISBN: 0996353003
ISBN 13: 9780996353007
LA Authentic Media: Los Angeles, Ca.
PostGamePass.com

Disclaimer

Some names and identifying details have been changed to protect the privacy of individuals.

Cover photo by Robert Ector

Table of Contents

Introduction

"This is a big boy's game."
—Spurs head coach Gregg Popovich,
Game 5 of the 2013 NBA Finals

Over the last two decades, the business of professional sports has undergone tremendous transformation. In the eighties, the rise of cable TV created another platform for sports to grow its audience. Teams like the "Showtime" Lakers upped the entertainment factor at sporting events by infusing the Hollywood experience with the hardwood. The Lakers were the first to put celebrities courtside for games and to include in-game entertainment featuring a dance team. Owner Dr. Jerry Buss is also responsible for creating the postgame experience with the introduction of the Forum Club inside the arena for postgame partying.

In the NFL, two football dynasties captured the heart of America in the San Francisco 49ers and Dallas Cowboys. The Niners won five Super Bowl championships between 1981–94, while the Cowboys ruled the '90s, winning three titles between 1992–95 while featuring some of the brashest personalities in sports.

During this same time frame, as hip-hop took command of pop culture, we watched the ascension of Michael Jordan, and his relationship with Nike set the stage for a new athlete prototype.

The nineties ushered in the Allen Iverson era, ballooning salaries and the game changer, the Internet. Together, this set the stage for the creation of the new millennial athlete.

Today's athletes have grown up in the shadow of six-time NBA champion and brand icon Michael Jordan. Mix that with the allure of rapper/business entrepreneur Jay Z, and you have the ultimate mixture of superstar icon. This has created a savvy combination, as new millennial athletes are more aware of the benefits and pitfalls to being labeled a "brand" than ever before. The exchange for this higher level of notoriety is more scrutiny.

We've seen many examples of how the money and fame can vanish faster than a fifteen-second Snap Chat video. In these fast times, there's little patience for the growth and development process that is inevitable.

People make mistakes. Players fuck up.

As famous as Michael Jordan was, he never had to worry that someone in a casino or fast food spot had a cell phone documenting his every move. Things are different. Sports has become the ultimate reality show.

Athletes are our modern-day fables. Like the Greek heroes in those stories, we see the pros' tragedies and triumphs played out in real time. Often their escapades shift the entire conversation of the culture.

The story of how a hunter named Narcissus drowned in a puddle because he got so caught up staring at his own reflection can easily be a metaphor for any number of athletes who lost their careers by letting their "status" trip them up.

With the introduction of the Internet, the fourth wall was broken. Fans and their heroes were allowed access to one another like never before. For the fans, it was an opportunity to see everything: the good, the bad, and the outlandish. Things tend to look funny when you shine a brighter light on them.

The tagline for my website, JocksandStilettoJill.com, is "ESPN meets *Sex and the City*." It's the point where sports and the lifestyle meet up.

JSJ was born out of my love for sports and the connection they have to the culture at large. By far, the most sought-after stories on the site are the ones that delve into what happens once the athletes leave the stadiums and arenas. Whether it's hero worship, envy, or a cautionary tale, the culture of sports has everyone's attention.

Some of the questions I'm asked: Are things really that different from the golden era of professional sports? What motivates today's athlete? What type of money are they really making? Or, people are curious about simple things: Why do they date the same women? Why are a lot of those women strippers, bottle girls, and Internet starlets?

During my time working for corporate powerhouses like Nike, Sony Pictures Entertainment, Virgin Records, and BET Networks, I've had the opportunity to work with hundreds of athletes. Naturally, I developed personal relationships with some and along the way also connected with agents, executives, wives, groupies, and members of the entourage.

By default, I've become a curator of the culture. I've picked up on some patterns and been privy to stories that slipped under the radar of the blogs and SportsCenter.

I know you're interested, and I've got the answers. This book is your postgame pass to life after the final buzzer sounds.

Let's take a look at my view from the sideline:

CHAPTER 1

New Millennial Brand Athlete

E very athlete might not think they have the star power of Tom Brady or LeBron James, but today's athlete definitely believes they are a *brand*. It starts early; organizations are ranking athletes in the sixth grade. New millennial athletes are trademarking nicknames and catchphrases before they've laced up their sneakers or taken one snap in a professional game.

In a perfect world, a successful brand athlete will have a grasp on four main areas:

The Game: This is about talent and drive. He's reached the professional level; now what will he do to stay there? Of course there's always the added pressure of the newer, younger version of himself staring him in the face. Every season, there's another crop waiting to take his spot.

The Lifestyle: For some, this is the most difficult to navigate. Women, weed, and weather get them caught up every time. Missteps here kill careers.

The Business: Don't be delusional; professional athletics is a for-profit business first and foremost. It wasn't created for the owners to lose money. Players are the expendable pieces in all of this.

Jocks understanding how the corporate side of the game works and where he has leverage is key.

Postgame: These are the final seconds on the clock. A player better have an exit strategy and take heed of the red flags, so that he doesn't end up another example of wasted opportunity.

The window for the average pro athlete's career is small. The average NFL career is 3.5 years long, earning about $6.1 million. The average NBA player's career is 4.8 years and will earn $24.7 million.[1] Meanwhile the average Major League Baseball player will earn $17.9 million over an average of 5.5 years.

There are 1,696 spots in the NFL, 450 spots in the NBA, and 1,280 in the MLB. Those aren't huge numbers. It sounds cliché, but really, just making it is a huge accomplishment. But it doesn't end there. The goals are simple: become a star, win some shit, take advantage of some endorsement opportunities, and have a good time.

At any given time, the NFL, NBA, and MLB really only have five true superstars across each league. I use four areas to measure if an athlete qualifies for *Superstar Status:*

The Money: *Duh!* Like Cuba Gooding Jr. said in Jerry McGuire, "Show me the money." If the coins aren't there, the hype won't be, either. Teams are investing huge dollars behind what they consider "franchise players." It's basic math, plus common sense; if I pay more for it, it holds more value.

Rings: Wins matter. It is why they play the game. Leagues draft on potential, but the expiration date on that is short. That's not to say there aren't superstars without rings, but it does place them on a different rung.

---

1 http://www.businessinsider.com/chart-the-average-nba-player-will-make-lot-more-in-his-career-than-the-other-major-sports-2013-10

Social Currency: This is cultural and global appeal. Is an athlete hot in the streets? Of course there are different streets. But when you look at social currency, it's about a player's status, credibility, and universal adoration. This is the area that will enhance his legacy.

Significant Other: Let me keep it one hundred, it's hard for an athlete to be considered a superstar with a subpar boo at his side. When he can have his pick of the best and brightest, it seems logical that he can find a heart of gold in the body of a goddess, with a face to match.

Before we dig into the lifestyle, let's start off with a reminder. Not all professional athletes are created equal. There are obvious differences, like rookie or vet, but even within that, there's a pecking order in the system. Superstars are treated better than role players. That's not to imply role players are treated badly, but there are levels to this.

These are the categories of professional athletes:

Superstar: These are your top-tier guys. Along with all of the above, his days are split between being just your average pro athlete and being the face of a multimillion-dollar business brand. He's taking business calls during practice, on road trips he's filming his latest commercial, and on his off-days, he's booked for press and appearances. There is no off-season. Less downtime than your average pro. He's *busy* and the ultimate brand guy.

Star 1A: This is the guy that's almost at superstar status, but he's missing out on at least one of those key components listed above. He's Level 2, but enjoys similar superstar perks.

Rookie: This is just what it sounds like, the new or young guy on the team. This life is brand new. Every day is a new learning experience.

Midlevel/Role Player: This is the guy whose name and face aren't quite as known. They aren't the household name, but without them, there wouldn't be any teams or titles. Often they're the glue of the team. They make the machine work. Plus, by default, the natural celebrity of their career, and money, makes them pretty popular somewhere.

Vet: He's older, usually on the downside of his career, and is mainly around to add stability. He's seen the game from all angles; he gets his kicks laughing at the trouble the young pups get into. He's also there to offer guidance and wisdom.

Football vs. Basketball

You know the basic differences between football, baseball, and basketball. But are you aware there are also lifestyle differences? These are the ones you need to be aware of:

- The NFL is the most popular sport in America.
- The NFL has the shortest season, just sixteen games not including playoffs.
- NFL teams are given a "vacation" for one week during the season called a bye week. The NBA and MLB have All-Star breaks midway through the season. Both are about a week in length.
- NFL players' routines are highly regimented by their teams during the season. Unlike the NBA and MLB, NFL players have less time to get out and explore cities while they're on road trips. Most NFL teams have game-night curfews.
- NFL teams are rarely in a city for longer than a night. You won't catch NFL players hosting parties in the opposing team's city the night before a game like you do with the NBA. Tuesdays are their day off during the season, so Sunday and Monday nights are the nights you're most likely to catch them hanging out.

- The NFL's preferred off-season cities to train in are Miami, LA/Southern California area, and Phoenix/Glendale area. A lot of that has to do with the fact that the NFL's off-season typically begins at the end of January in the dead of winter. The athletes want to be somewhere warm and sunny. There are other reasons as well, but we'll get into that later.
- MLB has the longest season, running from early April to late September. They also have the most games at 162. They also have the most free time while on the road.
- Wondering which sport gives an athlete the highest probability of making it? Baseball.
- MLB off-season training destinations: Arizona, Florida.
- The NBA is more popular internationally than the NFL.
- The main NBA off-season training cities: LA, Vegas, Houston.
- Baseball players are harder to spot. They're generally of average height and build. NBA players are usually the easiest to spot and have the most face recognition, due to height and visibility on the bench. Plus there are only fifteen guys max on a roster. Even the last guy on the bench is a star to someone.
- NFL team's rosters contains a crowded fifty-three players, including the practice squad. NFL players have the hardest time being recognized. On any given Sunday, those guys are all wearing helmets on the sideline, which equals little to no face recognition value.
- The byproduct of that, football players tend to have helmet head syndrome. They do the most when they go out; it causes them to show off because they require more attention. That's who you'll spot in the club taking off his shirt. When bling was in, it was nothing to see some faceless, no-name guy barely hanging on to his NFL life, rocking an iced-out chain with a number he's only worn for two seasons. Their insecurity levels are a tad higher than NBA and MLB players.
- NFL contracts aren't guaranteed; only the signing bonus is. That means each season you face the potential of being cut,

with no financial impact to the team. Both MLB and NBA contracts are guaranteed. MLB players make the most money.

Now that you understand the lifestyle differences between the sports, let's look at the supporting cast of characters. Sure, we know his family and agent make up the inner circle, but there are many others who join in the process to make the machine run. These are the additional people you'll encounter in a professional athlete's entourage:

Professional Friends: Snoop Dogg and the Dogg Pound sang about it in the nineties. "It ain't no fun if the homies can't have none." What fun is a journey if you can't share it? These are the people you can expect to find in a jock's life.

First up, the Tommy and Cole to his Martin. Or, Turtle, E, and Johnny Drama to his Vinny Chase. For you throwbacks, Jerome to his Morris Day.

The goal is to flip the opportunity, like the "Four Horsemen" that's LeBron James and his close-knit group of friends-turned-business-partners.

Maverick Carter created LRMR, a marketing and management agency where he's rubbing elbows with Warren Buffet and producing TV and films.

His boy Rich Paul went from promoting and attempts at modeling, to becoming a certified sports agent, opening Klutch Sports Group with a client list that includes; King James, Tristian Thompson and Eric Bledsoe. The final piece, Randy Mims who handles travel and logistics.

But most professional friends aren't that skilled or lucky. Instead they get to live life as "do-boys." They lack ambition, becoming comfortable in the role of celebrity via affiliation.

The do-boy is basically the runner. He's picking up dry cleaning, holding the weed, or retrieving the car from valet after the club.

Professional friends take their role very seriously. They'll say things like, "I'm who makes sure he wakes up in the morning," or, "I get him to practice on time." These guys speak a lot of French. "*We* are headed to the playoffs." "*We* just got traded." "*We* are going on vacation."

Usually, there's no salary attached to this role. The benefits? Wearing his chain, shoes, or even an outfit. Access to the hottest parties, great game seats, plus basking in the jock's aura by association.

This guy can be a friend or actual family member.

That Guy That Plays Ball Overseas or Football in Canada: He's the ex-athlete that didn't make it. He might have even been drafted at one point. He was NICE in high school or college. Currently he's trying to figure out a hustle for himself. This guy usually morphs into one of two characters, after life smacks him with reality a few times. He either becomes a trainer, or an AAU coach. This friend often mistakes the jock's glory as his own success...

Cleanup Guy: The cleanup guy is really just around for the women. He's the one that's waiting to get on whatever's left over after Mr. Pro Athlete has made his selection. He is *super* nice to the random women. He sympathizes with the groupies' position. He sees the dirt that these guys do, so he'll even give a girl the scoop if he thinks it means he has a shot at her

He will be the one to try to convince a girl that the bedroom down the hall, not the master bedroom, is the place where all her dreams can come true. Unfortunately, he usually doesn't have a life plan and is really doing the same thing that the average groupie has set out to do, live off his boy. In his mind, he's equal to Mr. Pro Athlete because they may have sexed a few of the same women. If you don't have a problem waiting for your guy to ask Mr. Professional Athlete for funds to make a move, you can ball out with lowered expectations. His position isn't secure, either. He could get rolled out of the entourage at any given moment.

Rapper/Actor/Model/Comedian: There's always the friend that's going into entertainment. He's a "slash." He considers himself a hybrid: rapper/actor/model. Whatever gets his foot in the door, and some popularity by extension. He does it all. His motto when he wakes up: record every day, get features, and most importantly, when you meet celebs, get their e-mail addresses so you can connect and network.

Then there are the male groupies who really don't have a purpose. They're just there for the turn up and perks. Sometimes they get traded between jocks and celebrity entourages. By that point, they've outlived their usefulness with Jock A and move on to Jock 2B. These are the guys who always post photos to Instagram with athletes but don't even have their numbers.

Wife(y) vs. Fun Girl: Some women are meant to be the *wife*, while others are meant for a good time. And sometimes the good time can win out over a good and stable home. *Yes*, athletes like strippers, Instagram starlets, and girls that do something "strange" for a piece of change.

The average athlete works for maybe four hours a day. Once the season starts rolling, that time is cut down even more. That's a lot of free time. There are only so many hours you can spend in the gym or watching game film. He's going to find something to do with all that spare time.

A flexible schedule is definitely an asset. This is where strippers and Instagram models have the advantage over a regular girl. Accessibility and availability are important. While the nine-to-five girl is punching the clock, putting in a hard day's work, the bottle girls and Instagram vixens are at home, ready to "come through," at a moment's notice. Yes, there are times when a scantily clad chick with twenty-five thousand followers, will be more important than the college-educated girl next door.

The fun girls, groupies, party girls, whatever name you give them, represent the idea of a stress-free good time.

Escorts and prostitutes figure into this equation as well. Athletes pay for it because they aren't looking for long-term situations. An athlete is in town, and simply wants to interact. They aren't just paying for easy sex; they're also paying for discretion and the ability to ditch the woman as soon as they're ready with no headaches.

In a lot of ways, the introduction of a girlfriend into an athlete's life can cause issues for the professional friend. First, he might have to move out if she moves in or becomes a permanent fixture at the house. The introduction of a steady girlfriend puts an end to the spontaneous turn up. A girlfriend cuts into some of the friend's use. That could mean one less vacation in the off-season because the jock is going to want to spend quality time with his boo and less money toward the friend's day-to-day living expenses. For many professional friends, a new girlfriend represents the potential for a hostile takeover. Someone that threatens his position.

When he get on, he's gone leave your ass for a white girl
Is there a preferred look? Yes!

Everyone has their preference, but one quick perusal through any athlete's social media account will tell you all you need to know about that athlete's "type." There's definitely a preference for "exotic" among some athletes. It doesn't mean that they don't date, love, and lust after black women, but the desire to try something different is hard to overlook when it's so available. Generally it's more about a "look," but for some, race does factor into it. By the numbers, black professional athletes marry black women at a rate of 72 percent.

That mean's at least three-fourths of the time, it's intra-racial. But that number is still well below the average for black men who make over $100,000 a year, at 83 percent, and the national average of 88 percent for black marriages[2] overall.

These are the other people you are likely to encounter in today's athlete's entourage:

The Investment Guy: Someone is always trying to sell a pro athlete something. Condos in Miami, a new energy drink, a clothing line, etc. The investment guy knows just enough of everyone and has had some success in the past, so he's inclined to believe that he will again. He always has a plan to secure some sort of funding from the athlete. He'll pay for a nice dinner, though.

Jewelry Guy: Somebody has to supply athletes with their watches, chains, and sparklers.

Stylist/Lifestyle Guru: Everybody is a cool kid when it comes to athletes. They all have developed a "look" and are red carpet ready.

Publicist/Branding Specialist: This is the person who will take over an athletes social media accounts after he tweets five too many inappropriate things. E-mail the blogs, book him on radio and TV, and convince him that he need a web series.

Promoter: Nightlife is extremely important. If an athlete isn't hooked in with the right promoter, he could be left standing outside his favorite club with all the pedestrians. The promoter can also make the athlete a little side money if they're into "hosting" a club night. Although some guys do it just for the table and bottle service.

---

2 http://www.essence.com/2011/08/15/real-talk-are-you-giving-up-on-black-love/

The Friend That Does Security: Depending on their status, most athletes aren't hiring day-to-day security. Perhaps for a big night out at the club, but that's not something they generally spend money on. What you will see is that one friend or homie who has assumed the role of security in the crew.

Another professional friend you should get familiar with is the one that's there for the athlete's protection. He's a little different from the guy that does "security."

This is the guy in a city that's connected to the streets. He makes sure that the rest of the city's thugs fall back. In some form or fashion, this guy is getting broke off. And you'll see him with multiple athletes and crews. Is he just that cool? He just might be, but more important than that, he's going to make sure they move through the city with no problems.

One notorious "protector" put together an AAU team. The team wasn't sponsored by any of the NBA players that grew up in the city, but from a guy who frequented the city in the summer. The "sponsorship" had nothing to do with a desire to give back to the community, but more to do with the fact that he needed to avoid getting his chain snatched again.

Friend of the Hoes: This can be a male or female whose usefulness is tied to them always knowing the "bad chicks." The halo effect in that women always want to be around this individual because they know that they are the golden ticket to partying with the pros.

This is the friend a jock calls when he's really trying to turn up in a city. Or if he's having a private soiree at the house. You want to know why all the bad chicks on social media end up linking up and becoming friends? It's because always having a new girl to bring to the party is of value. It's their ticket in the door.

Now that you understand who all the key players are, we've come to my first piece of advice for finding success as a professional brand athlete: find a mentor.

CHAPTER 2

Warm-up

Stepping into the professional leagues is a grown man's arena. Draft day is actually the beginning of the cycle. They're going from the top of the heap back to the bottom again. The next level means everybody is as good as he is, except now they're also bigger and the game speeds up. Teams have their own identities and culture requirements that are unique to them.

Anytime you're placed into a new environment, you'll be faced with an assortment of personalities, politics, and procedures that you'll need to learn to navigate. The habits developed in the early stages of a career set the stage for how the athlete will be viewed in the future.

The new millennial athlete was coddled early because of his athletic ability. Just because his talent was enough to get him to the professional level doesn't mean the maturity is there to match. In this new era, professional head coaches have to do things like schedule room service to his players' rooms on the road to make sure they wake up in time for shoot around. Or they're giving out assigned seats on charter flights like the jocks are kids in grade school.

Studies show that most people who succeed in life have a mentor. Vets become like surrogate dads, uncles, "Big Bro," teaching the rookies the ways of the lifestyle. The little stuff factors in more than you can imagine.

A bit of guidance isn't a bad thing. Mentoring has been associated with higher job satisfaction, higher promotion rates, higher future income, and increased work success.

Some rookies will be experiencing their first extended stay away from home. They get homesick. Mentors might even help with basic things, like a kid from California not knowing the proper coat to buy for winter.

Or they need assistance adjusting to the professional league schedule. You always hear stories about young guys hitting the rookie wall because of the added number of games and nonstop travel. That can be both physically and mentally draining.

Then you have the rookies who just want to party, meet girls, and enjoy the fruits of their labor. Yes, it's a huge accomplishment to have made it to the professional ranks. But that's just step one of the journey.

The flip side to that energy is where your veterans come into play. They've been there, done that. They are usually more focused on winning because they're all partied out. Their focus might be on ensuring the paychecks keep rolling in, while young players are generally more concerned with proving that they belong in the league and establishing some sort of legacy.

Athletes are sensitive. They fear being second. If you hear a guy say he thinks Baller A is a much better player than him, I guarantee you he's being fake humble or he's not a winner. I'm not talking about mutual respect and admiration.

But that doesn't mean that you won't go through those moments of self-doubt. Having someone who's experienced it through a similar lens is an asset.

The Media

Jocks and the media have a love-hate relationship. They need each other, but it's complicated. Don't believe an athlete when he says he doesn't watch analysis shows, keep up with "hot takes," or read the news—that includes blogs. They all do. And at times it gets into their heads and affects their game.

Some athletes feel the media is full of those who couldn't make the cut at the professional level, so they settle for writing and critiquing. Or, if it's ex-athletes doing the analysis, the standard line is usually that said athlete is trying to stay relevant or they're mad because their time has passed. The general sentiment is that the media can never give a fair assessment.

Coming off his 2014 NBA MVP, Kevin Durant seemed to be working through being a brand and balancing that with personal growth. He became tired of being a PC player, acting like he didn't go through things and grapple with emotions. He spoke about his early years in the league when he was "finding himself" and focused more on being what everyone told him to be. He blamed that on the media.

"To be honest, man, I'm only here talking to y'all because I have to," *Durant said. "So I really don't care. Y'all not my friends."*[3]

In a November 2014 *ESPN the Magazine* cover story, New York Knicks star Carmelo Anthony talked about dealing with the media:

3 http://bleacherreport.com/articles/2365532-kevin-durant-comments-on-relationship-with-media-at-2015-nba-all-star-weekend?utm_source=twitter.com&utm_medium=referral&utm_campaign=programming-national

"As an athlete, you don't really have a voice," he says. "Everything you say or do, people have a million opinions about it, so it doesn't really get heard the way you want it to get heard. People are putting things on you and shaping your reputation, and you don't really have control."

The strong ones learn how to either embrace the added scrutiny or block it out. After a while, the critiques start to blur together, and a resistance is built up. They seemingly become immune.

Separation Anxiety: Trades

When a trade happens, that is when athletes usually learn that sports is a business. When trades take place during the off-season, the athlete has an easier time adjusting. They have time to become familiar with the team staff, get the opportunity to study a new playbook, and learn their way around a new city.

When trades happen in-season, things move at a quick pace. A jock will have to get to his new city within a day or two. That means extended hotel living. It doesn't just end there; he will still need to find somewhere to live on a permanent basis. Packing up the old spot becomes the job of family, the girlfriend, or professional friends.

Trades bring about major change to the pros' environment. It can be emotionally difficult for those who have developed brotherhood-type camaraderie.

The OKC Thunder experienced that heartache two seasons in a row.

In 2011 the trade between the Boston Celtics and the Thunder was pretty rough on a young Thunder team. They traded up-and-comer Jeff Green for veteran big man Kendrick Perkins. The trade was needed to get OKC over the hump, but the toll it took on the athletes was obvious.

Green looked miserable on the Celtics bench for weeks following the trade. In the immediate aftermath, the Thunder teammates found out the news as they were on a bus. The team was reportedly unusually silent in the aftermath. They were sad and missing their friend…and then it happened again.

Unable to reach an extension agreement with 2012's NBA Sixth Man of the Year, James Harden, the Thunder traded the guard to the Houston Rockets. The surprise move happened on a Saturday night; Kevin Durant was at a college football game when he got the news that Harden's tenure with the Thunder came to an end. KD left the game because he was so upset at the news.

The added benefit of social media is getting to see athletes' reactions to these types of scenarios in real time. Several players tweeted in disbelief that the Thunder let go of the rising superstar. Harden was at dinner with his family when he received a text from Thunder general manager Sam Presti, telling him that he loved him and things just didn't work out.

At times, the loss of a teammate can seem like a death in the family. That's no exaggeration; in 2004 Cuttino Mobley was traded from the Orlando Magic to the Sacramento Kings. Cuttino and his BFF at the time, Steve Francis, spent six seasons playing together as members of the Houston Rockets. They were later traded to Orlando together.

Twenty-three games into the season, and just before tipoff, the Magic dropped the bomb that Cat was traded for Doug Christie. The move sent Francis into an emotional whirlwind that included Francis saying he was "drained and distracted" while playing in the game following the news that Mobley was traded. Francis was upset that Cuttino was alerted thirty minutes before tipoff.

Steve later went deeper into his feelings about the move, saying:

"I can't put it into words," he said. "Playing with a guy, living with a guy, just knowing that every day when I wake up that's something I can count on, that I'm going to be in practice or in a game with Cuttino.

"Him not being here is going to be tough for me. I don't know what I'm going to wake up for."

Real.

In 2010 after LeBron James left Cleveland to become a champion in South Beach, his former Cavs teammate Mo Williams took his departure extremely hard. Mo logged into Twitter at 1:00 a.m. to release his emotions. As each tweet passed, it seemed as if Mo was on an emotional roller coaster equivalent to a really bad breakup.

First he seemed angry and desperate. Looking for answers by questioning everything he once believed in:

"I can't believe this is really real. This is surreal. So many emotions on one man decision. I wonder what is our next move. 1:38 a.m."

Then, the depression began to sink in. The realization that the relationship is over:

"The only thing, and I mean the only thing I disagree with is…If he knew somewhere else was the destination. He should have spared cle 1:43 a.m."

Next Mo seemed to be searching for something to hold on to. Something to believe in:

"Love u bron and always will. I know u made your decision for the rt reason but we could have got it done here and u would have enjoyed it in cle a whole lot more. But I have no idea what went on

behind closed doors but I can sit here today and say that I am truly blessed 1:46 a.m."

Finally, Mo seemed to find hope in the power of positive thinking.

"Well, after I wake up in the morning its a new day and I can embark on the new journey in my life. Love all my fans. But we will make it thru. 2:25 a.m."

But, that didn't last long before it was back to the denial stage:

"The person that I feel most sorry for is mike brown. He is a really good coach. 2:28 a.m."

Williams said it took him a long time to get over the pain of losing LeBron. When the Heat lost to the Dallas Mavericks in the 2010 NBA Finals, Mo tweeted that Dallas had healed his heart.

Once the jock becomes familiar with the routine, understanding how to manage his body, and team politics, the next level he has to master is "the life."

CHAPTER 3

The Life
The Game Away from the Game

There will always be that one teammate that orchestrates the fun. He's the chief minister of foolishness, and his house is the designated fun zone. I call his spot the "boom boom room." You automatically know that if this guy is involved, debauchery is sure to follow.

He's the teammate that will fly in "talent" from other cities to entertain for a special occasion, or just because the team has become bored with the local work. Basically, he imports the strippers or the fun girls that like to party. This can go down either at home or on the road. On the plus side, he's also often the guy that can rally the teammates or play peacemaker in any locker room beefs.

Let's take the example of former Minnesota Viking Frank Smoot. Back in 2005 he had a "love cruise" complete with strippers/prostitutes, alcohol, and all the X-rated things you can imagine. The love cruise scandal was a party thrown on two rented houseboats. Several members of the Vikings were present, as well as women flown in from Atlanta and Miami. The crew of the ships reported witnessing several sex acts and having to clean up used condom wrappers, K-Y Jelly, and sex toys the following day.

Fred Smoot later said in an interview that too much was made out of the sex on the love cruise. That the whole experience was "overrated."

Double-headed dildos and oral sex is pretty self-explanatory, no?

Road Trips

It's almost mandatory when a team hits a city that someone on the team (usually a vet) arranges a night out. Players' going out together creates team bonding. When guys enjoy one another's company, the chemistry flows. That's not to imply that people can't simply work together and keep it moving. But often times these team excursions lead to improved play. Shaq used to call these nights out while on the road "team meetings."

Some "team meetings" start with dinner. Usually different players will invite a mixture of friends who are known fun girls, investment guys, and friends of the hoes. It ensures that dinner is visually appealing; plus, it offers some of the younger, less experienced guys an early opportunity to secure a date for the night and avoid scraping the bottom of the barrel with roadkill. This is important because some cities are notorious for their lack of "quality work."

After dinner it's time to hit the club. If it's one of *those* nights, bottles and sparklers are definitely on the agenda. Generally players take turns buying table service, unless the athlete is hosting, in which case the bottles are on the house. Some nights they'll split the cost of bottle service.

Bottle service is a "VIP" experience, where the club provides bottles of alcohol, a dedicated bottle girl, and VIP seating. As the bottles are brought out, some sort of light display is created for effect, to let everyone in the club know that there's big money in that area.

Depending on the city—and the time of year—a table can run a guy anywhere from $2,500 for a bottle or two to about $20,000–$30,000 in Las Vegas or Miami during a fight weekend or Memorial Day. Even a day party in LA during the summer can hit you for $15,000–$20,000 on a regular weekend. Don't forget the 20 percent tip at the end of the night.

You've heard stories of rookies and younger players assigned "hazing" tasks from the vets. Sometimes it's simple stuff like donning a Dora the Explorer backpack or early-morning food runs before practice.

But at times, they have additional responsibilities on the road. For example, the young guys hold on to the condoms for the married players of the team. Can't let wifey find a used condom wrapper in your travel kit. Plus the young guys are more likely to be single, with no one to answer to.

A sturdy veteran presence on a team is often a key piece to a winning formula. Someone that helps maintain balance and order in the locker room. The vet will be the guy who rounds his teammates up when it's time to leave the club so they're rested enough and on time for shoot around or the game the next day.

Veteran NBA player Chauncey Billups took on this role when he was with the Denver Nuggets following the trade of Allen Iverson to the Pistons. Billups was a finals MVP in 2004. He came to a Nuggets team that had been influenced by AI's partying. That team consisted of Carmelo Anthony, JR Smith, and Kenyon Martin to name a few. It's no secret that those guys enjoyed the nightlife, but one word from Billups and they would wrap things up. Billups also had an impact on how some of those guys stepped up their pregame wardrobes. Billups set the example of how a professional should carry himself.

Vets also provide valuable assistance in other areas. For example, teaching players how not to get caught up when they are giving multiple women game tickets.

The hours in the locker room before the game can be used in a multitude of ways. Some guys focus on the matchup ahead, reading scouting reports or watching film. Some are glued to their phones, texting, tweeting, and doing it for the Vine.

Then there's the other group of guys who are dealing with the game within the game. Tickets and seat locations.

There's a myth that players don't have to pay for tickets to the games. That they can just ask and receive any number of tickets and they don't have to spend any money for them. False.

For home games, players are given two season tickets in a designated area of the arena or stadium. If players want more tickets or an upgrade, like courtside seats, they have to purchase those seats at a discounted rate.

So that means if you're a jock and you have your main and a mistress attending your game, you have to make sure that those seats don't end up next to each other. Home games, it's easier to manage. There's usually a family section for tickets. Of course the main girlfriends and wives are always scanning that area, looking for any women they feel are showing off or cheering extra hard for their man.

But on the road, it's different. And in most situations, visitors' tickets are seated together. That could make for some pretty awkward situations.

In order to ensure that doesn't happen, teammates will switch tickets with one another. The tragedy that can come from two ladies crossing paths and cheering for the same guy is the type of stuff that leads to nude photo leaks or subliminal tweets and Instagram posts.

But there's more to it than that. It also means somebody is going to be left out. That means no postgame passes.

After a game, players hit the locker room, talk with the coaches, deal with media, shower, and if there's time, they visit with friends and family who attended the game.

That's where the postgame pass comes in. A section of the stadium or arena is designated for players to say quick hellos, flick up, and connect with friends and family for a few minutes before they board the team bus to catch their charter flight to the next city.

Even if an athlete leaves a girl tickets to the game, depending on her status, he might not leave her a pass to see him before he leaves town.

It could be because they have their main chick in town. There are certain cities the wives make it a point to travel to with their significant other, just in case bae, or a particular groupie, has plans to be Mrs. Professional Athlete 2B on the road. But we'll get into that topic later.

Even if the main girlfriend isn't in town, maybe the girl is merely roadkill—a random girl who is available for sex, but not someone he's interested in. Why would they want their friends and family to be potentially exposed to her? Can't take the chance that she will try to befriend Mom or his agent's daughter.

But some ladies picked up on that. They started coming prepared. For example, most NBA teams don't update their visitor passes. The only recognizable difference is the date stamp. Everybody has access to a color scanner and top-flight arena security isn't always on their game.

Contrary to the myth, jocks really don't mind if a woman has been with another athlete. Groupies don't really exist, only "bad bitches." She has twenty thousand followers on Instagram and gets mad likes, that's a trophy. It's about ego.

Most teammate beefs start over three things: money, status, and women.

CHAPTER 4

Recycling

*"People don't understand the mentality of a professional
athlete. He wants to conquer everything in front of him.
On the court, at the club, when he sees something he
wants, he goes after it. Whether he gets it or not, is a
whole different thing, but the mindset is still the same."*
—Eric Williams, retired NBA player

Life is easier when someone gives you a blue print to navigate your
way through. It's like that with jocks, too. Imagine living city to
city, sometimes making that change yearly, and while having to
find places to live, where to get your hair cut, and what spot has the
best big booty strippers, all on your own. Let's not forget you have to
do this while living up to your multimillion-dollar contract.

That's taxing!

They Love a Referral

That's why athletes love referrals. Think about it. You've noticed that
athletes frequent the same custom car dealers and jewelry guys, use
the same stylist or the super important tattoo artist. All those things
are important components of "the lifestyle." Not only do these items
announce that the athlete has arrived to the pro ranks, it's also about
peer approval.

What? You thought all that competitive energy stopped once they stepped off the field? Not a chance.

Have you ever listened to a couple of jocks having a conversation? They go something like this: "Ay, dog, you got that car? Me too! You copped that watch? Me too. You sexed that girl? ME TOO..."

Yes, they secretly *like* dealing with the same girls. Don't get it twisted; jocks want to be Mr. Popular, too. And nothing says I'm "swagging" all the way over you like pulling recycled premium talent and then flossing her over a teammate or fellow professional athlete.

For the insecure jock, it might get him props for being affiliated with top-notch box. Especially if he has a history of pulling duds.

Athletes compare women and judge teammates on the quality of women they can pull. They also happily swap stories about various women's sexual performance, along with whatever else they can relate to the desirability of the women.

Dr. J: *"Groupies are a necessary stress reliever."*

In his 2013 autobiography, Julius "Dr. J" Erving recounted[4] the story of his relationship with Samantha Stevenson. Stevenson is the mother of his thirty-two-year-old love child, tennis pro Alexandra Stevenson. Samantha was a freelance reporter that Dr. J met in the seventies while playing for the Sixers.

Dr. J described Samantha as a "hippie" with an "available vibe." That statement says love for free, right?

But everything has its price, and so did this. Dr. J said he used to chill at Samantha's house after games to unwind if he was feeling

---

4   Dr. J: The Autobiography

antsy or stressed. She became the Dr.'s "head doctor," supplying him with oral sex.

Dr. J recalled that the one time he had actual intercourse with Samantha was right after she got braces, so oral sex was a no-go. That one night led to her ending up pregnant. At the time, Dr. J was married to his first wife, Turquoise Erving.

Samantha and Dr. J reached an agreement that stipulated he dish out a hefty monthly stipend in exchange for Samantha's silence. Samantha got sole custody of Alexandra and had to live at least two hundred miles away. Samantha agreed because she didn't want to tarnish Dr. J's image.

"Groupies" are a necessary evil. Like a muse, they can release the tension following the physical and mental strain of competing in a professional sports environment. They also provide athletes with a common bond or forge a full-scale, level-10 beef.

Back in the nineties, it was rumored that superhot R&B singer Toni Braxton of "Unbreak My Heart" fame killed the future dynasty hopes of the Dallas Mavericks.

At the time, the Mavs featured a trio of Jason Kidd, Jimmy Jackson, and Jamal Mashburn. So the story goes, Toni was set to go out on a date with Jason Kidd. She went to the team hotel to meet up with him, but somehow ended up meeting Jason's teammate, Jimmy Jackson. She ditched her plans with Kidd and went out with Jimmy.

Kidd and Jackson were already having issues meshing on the court. Add in the drama of competing for a woman, the results could be bad. The two were traded from the Mavs a short time later, and both have denied the validity of that story. *But*, it wouldn't be the first or last time something like this caused friction on a professional sports team.

The benefits of the referral plan also have to do with comfort levels. The jock has access to her HoFax. That's sort of like Carfax, where you can get the background information on a used car you were planning on buying. A Carfax details any accidents or damage you need to be aware of before making that purchase. With a HoFax, a chick's entire history is run down from one player to the next.

Athletes tend to have a lot of time after practice. NBA players are only in practice a few hours per day; NFL practices are generally longer. While they're sitting in treatment or lifting weights, those are some of the conversations that are happening.

A jock will absolutely bust the bubble of his teammate to let him know he's not getting a fresh pair of Jordans out of the box with his latest boo.

The logic here is that the athlete is semiprepared for what to expect, should he decide to pursue or continue on with her. He'll know important traits like: Is she a thief? Does she have exceptional oral skills? Does she require gifts? Is she prone to stalk? After all, nobody wants to be robbed or played.

Time Out:

Earlier I mentioned that there are stories that don't always make it to the site. I'm going to share a few of these true stories with you throughout *PostGame Pass*, in the Time Out sections. Of course the names along with some of the details have been changed to protect the innocent and infamous.

Play #1: Don't be mad your chick chose me.

J was a second-year player stuck in a city that was dry as hell. Glued to the bench his rookie year, J's play improved his sophomore season, but he was stuck behind a vet so playing time was sparse. Lucky for J, he was traded from a team that was dying at the bottom of the standings to a playoff-bound team in a city known for its "quality work."

The "work" is how athletes refer to women that haven't earned a real place in the jocks' lives. They may text these women, and even hook up with them occasionally, but these are the situations that are likely going nowhere.

J had a girlfriend, but she was for the off-season. J made it his business to get familiar with the cities' most popular chicks, but he always abided by the rule "absolutely no wifing the work." You can't allow permanent feelings to invade a temporary situation.

One day J was in Target, picking up a few things when he ran into a "bad one" buying some sheets.

Her name was Alana; she was five foot six, cute shape, with hazel eyes and a fresh face. No makeup and most importantly to J, no weave.

J and Alana exchanged numbers and started hanging out. Alana had a great job, no Twitter, and wasn't on the scene. Hitting all those points was like discovering a diamond in the desert. *And* nobody knew her. Win. Jocks want to be explorers, too, uncovering new and uncharted territory.

Alana quickly became J's favorite…at least temporarily. J didn't want anything serious; plus his real girlfriend would be coming to visit soon.

One day J was in the weight room with Larry, one of his teammates. Larry had peeped J and Alana after a game or two and decided to ask J what was up with her.

J immediately went into story mode, sharing the recent nudes Alana had sent over to him and sharing that Alana was top-three head game. Typical weight room conversation.

J forgot about that convo, and eventually his girl came to visit a short time soon after. J forgot about Alana as he focused on wifey, and then, the next new chick that crossed his path.

Just before the start of the season, and around the holidays, jocks are prone to change their numbers. This can be for several reasons; I'll give you my top three:

1. He's not giving gifts and doesn't want to be asked for them—that goes for friends and family, too.
2. He's trying to shake some persistent young lady that doesn't understand he was just having fun. Meanwhile, she believes she's found the one that's going to make her turn in her hoe panties and settle down into a real relationship.
3. Or he got caught and wifey found out.

Whatever the case, it's not an uncommon occurrence. J changed his number, so there was no way Alana could get back in touch with him unless she was willing to put some effort behind it.

The next time J saw Alana, she was waiting postgame in the tunnel for his teammate Larry. J absolutely felt some type of way, but his pride wouldn't allow him to speak to her. J watched as Alana climbed into the passenger side of Larry's Range, and caught the smirk on Larry's face.

The following day in the locker room, J was telling his teammates how Larry was picking up his sloppy seconds. And how she was only messing with Larry because she couldn't have J.

Problem with that was the night before he was texting Alana, asking her why she was messing with that "clown" and didn't she miss him. Alana had no allegiance to J anymore, especially because Larry had shared with her the previous conversation he and J had about her. Alana forwarded Larry the screen shots of the texts…

Now the whole team knew that J would hate on his teammate just to get back in the good graces of a chick he had no real plans for.

Where J and your typical athlete mess up is they want to be known for having hoes, but not being a rest haven for them. J had shown off photos; he also shared how she stopped, popped, and dropped it. But when his teammate asked, "Is that you?" J let his ego get in the way, so he says nah because he doesn't want it to seem as if he were cuffing the work.

A teammate will absolutely try to hit your girl. And some of them will drop all your business to do it. Professional friends will do this, too, but their approach is different. Teammates can be malicious. He's like 50 Cent; he wants to let you know he's fucking your bitch. So he'll make sure to like her pics, tweet at her, and post photos.

J didn't realize it, but by advertising her assets yet distancing himself from the chick, he gave Larry the referral and the stamp of approval.

The same things J saw in Alana, Larry saw, too. Once J put the stamp on the particulars, it was time for Larry to make his move.

The reality is, once a woman dates one pro athlete, it's easy to get another one. That's the "Me Too" effect.

Now J is salty because his teammate pulled his B rotation chick and he wasn't quite finished with her yet. If he reacts, his teammates think he's a sucker for love.

Wanting to look like "he don't love 'em, just replace 'em" led to him losing one to the game.

The reverse to this game, teammate beefs about women can get players traded or cut. It can also impact future earnings. There are instances where teams have been all set to sign players to lucrative deals, only to discover that there are some serious issues with a key vet.

• • •

Need more proof that recycling is good for the professional athlete environment? Check this list of six-degrees of separation.

- Hello, Kim Kardashian! NFL running back Reggie Bush, Dallas Cowboy Miles Austin, and NBA center Kris Humphries.
- San Diego Padres' star Matt Kemp had a serious relationship with ex-NFL wide receiver Terrell Owens's former fiancé, Felisha Terrell.
- Matt, NBA star Kevin Durant, and ex-NBA player DeShawn Stevenson all dated actress LeToya Luckett.
- Ex-Laker and Knicks head coach Derek Fisher's ex-wife Candace once dated former NFL star running back Marshall Falk. They have a son together.
- Marshall Falk married comedian Martin Lawrence's ex-wife, Pamela Southall.
- Deion Sanders is dating Tracy Edmunds, who was married to nineties R&B superproducer BabyFace, and spiritually married to Eddie Murphy for fourteen days.
- Speaking of Eddie, his ex-wife Nicole was engaged to NFL analyst and talk show host Michael Strahan.

- Former NFL QB Matt Leinart has a son with ex-USC volleyball star Brynn Cameron. In 2013, Cameron gave birth to another son by Clippers star Blake Griffin.
- Boxer Sugar Ray Leonard's ex-wife Juanita married former MLB star Otis Nixon.
- Singer Tatyana Taylor was engaged to NBA player Brandon Jennings, but is now in a serious relationship with another NBA player, Iman Shumpert.

CHAPTER 5

Gambling

A nother solid piece of advice: don't try to hang with the vets, money wise. Arguments over money tend to escalate quickly, or leave athletes with broke pockets and hurt feelings.

For the ultracompetitive, gambling can be just another added layer of complicated habits that mimics the adrenaline rush of winning in sports.

Professional athletes spend a lot of time traveling. All those hours up in the sky at thirty thousand feet lead to a lot of leisure time. While some are listening to music, sleeping, or surfing the web, others are making and losing money gambling with teammates.

In 2011, Memphis Grizzlies teammates OJ Mayo and Tony Allen had a scuffle on the team charter. Mayo and Allen were playing in a card game. Mayo lost and owed Allen $7,500. In unsportsmanlike fashion, OJ refused to pay up. He then added to the situation by trash-talking Allen. Clowning his game and reminding Allen that he wasn't a lottery pick in the draft like OJ had been. Teammates attempted to intervene, but OJ kept going. Tony Allen was about that life. He decided enough was enough and punched OJ in the eye.

One of the most infamous incidents in NBA history began over a gambling debt. In December of 2009, Washington Wizards players

Gilbert Arenas and Javaris Crittenton made headlines after an argument on a flight ended with the two players bringing guns into the team's locker room.

The issue began days earlier on December 19, when the two argued on a team flight over a card game.

Gilbert wasn't actually involved in the bet, but stepped in to stop Javaris from berating teammate JaVale McGee about the money he won during the game. Crittenton was agitated because he had lost $1,100. Crittenton threatened to shoot Arenas.

Two days later at a Wizards practice, Arenas laid out four guns in front of Crittenton's locker with a note, *Pick 1, so the day you want to shoot me, let me know, I'll be ready to get shot.*

The news became public on Christmas Eve. Arenas was suspended for the majority of the '09–'10 season. He also pleaded guilty to the felony charge of carrying an unlicensed pistol outside of a home or business.

His career never recovered from this incident. The Wizards later traded Gilbert to the Orlando Magic, who used their amnesty clause on him. He played his last NBA game in 2012, but he's still collecting NBA checks.

The $62 million that was remaining on his contract was spread out over a few years with the amnesty clause. For the team it allows that salary to be effectively wiped from their books with no salary cap hit.

Crittenton was only twenty-one at the time of the incident. He was suspended for the rest of the season, and then cut. He never played in the NBA again.

As of 2015, Crittenton took a plea deal and is serving twenty-three years for the 2011 murder of a twenty-two-year-old Atlanta mother of four. Crittenton was accused of targeting a man he believed robbed him, but shooting her by mistake.

While out on bond for murder, Crittenton was arrested again and charged with being a member of a drug ring that was attempting to move four hundred *kilos* of cocaine and ten *pounds* of weed.

I'm sure former NBA commissioner David Stern had to be longing for the days when things were simple. Like New York Knicks legend Charles Oakley slapping up a player or two for failing to pay their "gentleman's bet."

Then there are those moments when the subject matter of a bet provides locker room entertainment.

During the Miami Heat's first NBA Championship run in 2006, teammates took cash bets on how fast the South Beach lifestyle would turn rookie Wayne Simien out. Simien was a devout Christian, but that didn't stop his teammates from wagering who could get him into the strip club first, and which fun girl would be the one to get him caught up. Simien retired from basketball in 2009 and became a minister.

Here's a quick look at some of professional sports' biggest high rollers:

Michael Jordan: Michael Jordan's gambling issues have been well documented. He once admitted to losing $165,000 during a heavy night of gambling at an Atlantic City casino in 1993.

Charles Barkley: The NBA Hall of Famer and two-time Emmy winner admitted in 2006 that he had lost over $10 million due to his ongoing gambling habit. That estimate included $700,000 bets during one Super Bowl and a $2.5 million loss during a game of blackjack. The Wynn hotel in Las Vegas sued him in 2008 for $400,000 in unpaid gambling debts.

Floyd Mayweather Jr.: They don't call Floyd "Money" just because of his undefeated record. The boxer loves to show off his betting slips on social media—only the wins, so who knows how much he really loses—but when Floyd wins, it's big. Floyd once showed off a winning slip of $1.4 million on a $720,000 bet he made on a Colts vs. Jags game.

Gambling stimulates the brain's reward system. It's easy to see why some of sports' most competitive personalities develop an affinity for it.

CHAPTER 6

Ego

"And that's around the time that your idols become your rivals / You make friends with Mike, but gotta A.I. him for your survival."
—DRAKE, "THANK ME NOW"

People herald the image of the golden boy athlete. The humble guy who isn't boastful and never shows up his opponent. The reality is, *ego* fuels athletes. It's one thing when we're talking about the competitive play between athletes on opposing teams; it's something else when that battle becomes internal with teammates and places teams in a vulnerable position.

There are tons of examples, but one scenario that repeats itself often occurs when a highly touted rookie steps into a superstar's locker room.

Kobe and Shaq Lakers Dynasty

The Kobe and Shaq feud had everything. Fame, money, power struggles, media bickering, police involvement, and battle raps. With Hollywood as the backdrop, this was a soap opera that played over eight years and three NBA championships.

Shaq and Kobe were on the Lakers together from 1996 to 2004. The simple breakdown of their issues: O'Neal felt Kobe was too selfish, and Kobe felt Shaq was lazy.

Kobe and Shaq operated in two totally different mind spaces. Shaq is an oversize kid whose sheer power and gracefulness made it difficult for other centers to match up against him. Shaq probably could've worked a little harder at taking care of himself and prolonged his career. At the very least, it might have spared him from those unremarkable last few years in his career that saw him bounce from Phoenix to Cleveland and finally end his career in Boston.

Kobe seemed born to be an NBA star, groomed early. Combined with his overarching will, Kobe believes in practice and discipline. Shaq being "lazy" was too much for Kobe.

Power struggles ensued. After three NBA titles, and a loss to Detroit in the 2004 finals, one of the greatest tandems in NBA history was broken up.

Shaq is an example of the league's proverbial big brother. It's a role he seemed to relish, even if at times the lil bro wasn't interested in being "big brothered." Penny in Orlando, Kobe in LA, even Shaq's relationship with DWade soured toward the end.

Sometimes that cycle will ironically repeat itself—Kobe and Dwight Howard's one season together on the Lakers comes to mind—and then there are the cases when it's not a youngster rebelling against mentoring, but the star battling to remain the number-one option.

In 1992 Larry Johnson and rookie Alonzo Mourning were teammates on the Charlotte Hornets. On the surface, Johnson appeared welcoming, but Johnson took moves to ensure Mourning knew his place. Johnson was the number-one pick by the Hornets in the 1991 draft and won NBA Rookie of the Year.

Mourning was selected second overall by the Hornets in 1992. Johnson allegedly taunted Mourning in the locker room, waving his Rookie of the Year jacket at him, telling him that if he were good enough maybe he'd get one.

For three years the two played together in Charlotte, while battling behind the scenes to be the face of the franchise. They were never able to connect on court. Both felt they deserved to have more shots. Alonzo Mourning was traded to Miami, and LJ ended up in New York.

The beef resurfaced in1998 when Miami and New York met up in the playoffs. With 1.4 seconds left in the game, Johnson and Mourning got physical in front of New York's bench.

At the time, Mourning claimed Johnson threw an elbow at his face. They threw a few punches, but none really connected. The fight itself is largely remembered because Alonzo dragged New York's head coach at the time, NBA analyst Jeff Van Gundy, around the court. Jeff was trying to stop the fight and somehow ended up wrapped around Zo's leg while he was going after LJ.

So far, we've talked about how athletes compete away from the game. But there are times when those testosterone-filled beefs spill over into the arena.

Basketball is probably the only sport that you can actually see the manifestation of those emotions explode during play. In football, for example, the players might both play offense on opposing teams. In that instance, two beefing jocks will never match up against each other on the field.

Baseball doesn't have as much physical contact—unless a player goes charging at the pitcher on the mound and teammates empty the dugout.

But in basketball, players are all on the court together, defenders switch positions, guys line up next to one another at the free-throw line, or get tangled up going for a rebound.

There is one NBA point guard who is known for hitting players in their naughty bits and asking them how they know his ex-girlfriend during the game. This happened during actual game play.

You're watching the game at home, and you see two athletes getting tangled up, you're thinking that's passion from the game. Competitors fired up in the heat of the battle. I'm wondering if they ever dated the same woman.

Time Out:
Playoff Problems

What type of beef happens when two players on conference rival teams face each other in the NBA Playoffs?

Wood and JT had leftover beef from All-Star Weekend. Both were dealing with the same girl from Chicago named Lynn. A former teammate of Wood's named Eric shared the connection with his new teammate, JT, after running into Lynn and Wood together during All-Star Weekend.

Both Wood and JT had serious relationships with long-term girlfriends.

When Wood found out Lee was dealing with JT, he immediately started talking shit about JT's hoop skills. Wood couldn't understand why Lynn would be dealing with a scrub. Wood was an All-Star; JT was still a young player trying to establish himself.

During the conference playoffs, JT's team was behind by a point with fifteen seconds left in Game 6. JT intentionally fouled Wood. The refs immediately called a foul.

But Wood was heated JT fouled him and pushed JT down onto the court. Wood was given a technical foul. Problem with that, Wood had been fired up all game. That was his second tech of the game, which resulted in an automatic ejection.

This was a closeout game for Wood's team. He let his ego get in the way, and his team ended up having to play a Game 7. All because he went "sensitive Smurf" over a girl.

But as professional teams have cut back on physical play, the beef has manifested itself in other areas.

Hip-Hop Beefs in Sports

Think about how hip-hop got involved with former Washington Wizards guard DeShawn Stevenson's beef with LeBron James.

During King James's first go-round in Cleveland, a conversation allegedly took place where he told his teammate Drew Gooden that Stevenson was all hype.

The comments made their way back to Stevenson. They struck a nerve. Stevenson shot back at LeBron, saying he was overpaid and wasn't Kobe.

LeBron fired back by dismissing DeShawn, saying, "For me to respond to him would be like Jay Z responding to a diss record by Soulja Boy." Fast-forward to the Wizards-Cavs playoff series...

DeShawn invites Soulja Boy to sit courtside at Game 3, a Wizards home game.

And then the impossible happened. A rapper/NBA minority team owner hopped on a track and dedicated three minutes to a basketball beef. Jay Z weighed in with a diss track dedicated to DeShawn Stevenson, using Too Short's "Blow the Whistle."

But, the really disrespectful part, when the hottest club in DC - Stevenson's team's city - "Love", played the record with Jay Z dissing the home team during the playoffs. And then, runs the track back.

You'd think that would be enough...but LeBron's teammate, Damon Jones, got on the mic and dissed Stevenson, before they dropped the song.

DeShawn's teammates were in the club and texted him.

Stevenson wanted the players to boycott the club. But an athlete not going out isn't realistic. A team rivalry rarely stops the party or the promoters.

Cleveland bounced DC out of the playoffs two years straight. In 2011, after LeBron took his talents to South Beach, the two met in the NBA Finals. DeShawn was playing for the Dallas Mavericks. The Mavs won the championship on the Heat's home floor.

You would think the Mavs would want to hop on their chartered flight and head back to Dallas to celebrate in their city. Nope, they stayed right there in Miami, partying at one of the Heat's favorite nightspots, Club Liv.

"OK, we poppin' Champaign like we won a championship game."— Lil Wayne "Pop Bottles"

The team rang up $110,000 at Club Liv inside Miami's Fontainebleau Hotel. And $90,000 of that tab was from a single bottle of champagne: a Nebuchadnezzar of Armand de Brignac— also known as the Gold bottle Ace Of Spades champagne. The fifteen-liter bottle is equivalent to twenty regular-sized bottles.

Mavericks owner Mark Cuban also left a $20,000 tip for the wait staff after partying with the team until 5:00 a.m. They headed back to Dallas early that morning.

Dsteve stepped off the plane that morning, rocking a T-shirt that said, "Hey, LeBron, tell me how my Dirk tastes." A reference to Shaq's infamous 2008 freestyle rap where Shaq asked Kobe how his ass tasted after the Lakers loss to the Boston Celtics in the 2008 NBA Finals.

But ultimately LeBron got the last laugh. In August 2013, DeShawn was on Twitter, trying to get a job with the Heat, and told LeBron to make it happen.

Athletes vs. Entertainers

Rapper Lil Wayne is a huge sports fan. You can always catch Wayne in attendance at some of the biggest sporting events. But back in 2013, Wayne claimed that someone in the NBA was holding him back. Wayne claimed both Oklahoma City and Miami didn't want him courtside at their games.

During All-Star Weekend in Houston, Wayne hosted "LIV on Sunday" at Stereo Live in Houston, Texas. With tons of celebrities in attendance like Giants WR Victor Cruz, Redskins WR Desean Jackson, Drake, J Cole, and Meek Mill, "Young Tunechi" launched into a rant about the NBA and the Miami Heat.

> "If you're wondering why you didn't see me at the All Star Game," Weezy began his rant, "it's because I was banned from attending all NBA events. The Miami Heat got me banned." He then led the crowd in a chant of, "Fuck NBA! Fuck Lebron! Fuck SheWade! Fuck Chris Bosh! And I fucked Chris Bosh wife!"

Of course the incident was recorded on multiple cell phones and went viral that same night. Months later during an interview with Jimmy Kimmel, Wayne was asked why he went off on the Heat like that.

Wayne's response was a sheepish, "I said that? I was too turnt up that night. I was a little too turnt up."

CHAPTER 7

Zero to One Hundred Real Quick-Nightlife and Strip Clubs

E veryone needs an outlet to unwind.

There are certain cities that athletes look for as soon as the schedules are set for the season. That's because these are the cities that contain the best of everything: women, nightlife, shopping, food, and training facilities. They are also where you'll find the largest concentration of athletes living in the off-season.

When wives and girlfriends travel with their men on road trips, these are the cities you're guaranteed to find them in.

These are also the cities that athletes can get caught up in whether they're just in town for the night or on vacation.

In no particular order, your favorite athlete's favorite cities:

Houston: In 2013 rapper Slim Thug's pitch to Dwight Howard during NBA free agency listed out all the virtues of the city that a single millionaire might be thinking about when selecting a new team. Better strippers, lower child support, and no state tax were the highlights of this uniquely tailored pitch. He also mentioned the cheaper bottle service and provided a referral to the cities local talent and popular Instagram vixens.

LA: Home of the three *W*s, women, weed, and weather. Playing in LA means instantly being a part of the Hollywood lifestyle. Every game, the celebrity row is filled with A listers; plus access to the best parties is in the middle of the workweek. It's also the second largest media market in the country, which means ample opportunity for paparazzi to catch them slipping.

Miami: Miami is another beast. South Beach offers year-round great weather and clubs that stay open until 5:00 a.m. The city is often referred to as the home teams' "sixth man" because athletes tend to get seduced by all the options available to them while there.

Shaq said in his 2011 book, *Uncut*, that he wasn't sure how the 2006 Miami Heat won the NBA championship that year because they "partied too fucking much."

Ask Siohvaughn Funches, the ex–Mrs. Dwyane Wade, or Shaunie O'Neal about the perils of Miami living

> *Miami is a great city[5]. It just wasn't a great city for our marriage. I know they say LA has its groupies, but Miami has a different mentality. Even going to the games, the whole environment is so different. Girls are practically sitting in their bra and panties in the arena. When you're trying to keep your husband, that's a lot to take. It was a whole new lifestyle I wasn't ready for.*

Toronto: Raptors fans and hockey fans really support their teams. Toronto is also home to what many consider the most beautiful women on the northern continent. The legal drinking age is nineteen, so those one-and-done athletes in the NBA can legally get

---

5 Shaunie O'Neal's comments in a 2010 *Essence* interview regarding her divorce from Shaq

loose. Paparazzi's aren't running rampant, and technically it's "foreign" soil, so all the women seem exotic. Plus, Drake reps it.

Atlanta: It seems like since the nineties, Atlanta has been heralded as the promised land. Then it was known as "Hotlanta," with the explosion of the urban music scene, taking off with labels like LaFace and So So Def.

Now Atlanta is known as "Black Hollywood" where it's home to the production of several TV shows—both reality and scripted—and also serves as the headquarters for Tyler Perry Studios, CNN, and Nickelodeon. On the sports side, Turner studios, NBA TV, and Inside the NBA also call ATL home.

Atlanta is also home to many rappers, and several athletes make it their off-season home. Much like Houston, the ATL has cheaper real estate and better strip clubs than some of the larger cities like NY and LA.

Strip Clubs

Strip clubs have become virtually mainstream at this point. There are dozens of songs paying tribute to strippers; we see them on reality shows or wifed up by actors and rappers. Teammates bond by hanging out together. Sometimes that's going to involve alcohol and scantily clad women. Going out to the club can be for celebration, a cure from boredom, or a pick-me-up after a bad loss. But when there's that much alcohol, money, and testosterone together in a crowded space, some nights things can get tricky.

During rookie orientation, both the NFL and NBA offer "life skills" seminars for the young players. In some actors will reenact real life situations that popped off in a club. They also have used role-playing to give the rookies a guideline on how to react to certain situations that might develop on a night out.

The cost of a night out at the strip club depends on the athlete. Should he decide to fall in love for the night with a dancer, he's going to have to pay for her time. One athlete confessed to me that he spent $25,000 a few nights in the strip club. He didn't consider that an outlandish number. NBA player Matt Barnes said that when he and Allen Iverson were teammates, AI would frequently drop between $30,000 and $40,000 on those nights in the strip club.

But every now and again, things can get out of control.

Adam "Pac Man" Jones can relate to that. In February 2007, the NFL cornerback was accused of starting a strip club brawl at Minxx during NBA All-Star Weekend. Pac Man made it rain on forty dancers with about $40,000. Somehow there was a miscommunication because Pac Man only intended to use the money as a prop, not to actually tip the dancers. Pac Man wanted his money back, and things got ugly.

An altercation took place that spilled outside the club. When it was all over, three people were shot, including a bouncer who was shot in the chest and forearm. He and Jones fought over him sweeping up the money. A shift manager was shot in the chest, and a woman attending the party was grazed in the head.

The NFL suspended Jones for one season. He also lost a civil suit two of the victims brought against him. He appealed and lost that also. In January of 2015, he was ordered to pay $12.4 million.

Athletes and strip clubs aren't a new phenomenon. Nineties basketball had its own strip club scandals. In 1999 an Atlanta strip club named the Gold Club would become the backdrop for a trial that involved a nice little mix of federal charges including racketeering, credit card fraud, prostitution, money laundering, and police corruption.

Gold Club owner Steve Kaplan was indicted on federal charges. In addition to Kaplan, one his most popular dancers, Jacklyn "Diva" Bush was also indicted and accused of being a prostitute. She was referred to as the "Michael Jordan of Sex."

The owner was accused of having Diva and other strippers sleep with the athletes as a perk. His big marketing idea was, if he provided athletes and celebrities with free sex, it would increase the club's profile and lure more people in to spend money. Rather genius if you think about it. Then the club would overcharge the clients on their credit cards. In Diva's book, *The Gold Club*, she revealed that dancers referred to athletes as "ATMs."

This all went down in private VIP rooms. Each room was fully stocked with women and alcohol. The anthem for those nights: "There are no rules tonight!" Dancers were paid $1,000 for sex acts, either with one another or with the athletes enjoying the adult entertainment. Sometimes the dancers would head over to the athletes' hotels for a private show.

The trial revealed the sex-capades of various athletes. Former Knicks legend Patrick Ewing had to take the stand and testify about his experience getting head from a stripper in one of the VIP rooms, while Kaplan watched.

Some of the names attached to the Gold Club Scandal include these stars:

Former Atlanta Falcon Jamal Anderson; former New York Knicks Patrick Ewing, Larry Johnson, John Starks, Dikembe Mutombo, Andrew Jones, Reggie Miller, Jerry Stackhouse, and Dale Davis; former Bronco Terrell Davis—no relation to Dale—and Dennis Rodman.

In 2007, Kaplan was sentenced to three years in prison; he gave up ownership of the Gold Club; paid a $5 million fine; paid back $250,000 to customers for credit card fees; had a restitution of $50,000 to Delta Air Lines; and had to forfeit $38,400 in cash grabbed during a government search.

In 2010 former Titans QB Vince Young had an unfortunate altercation at 3:00 a.m. inside Dallas's Club Onyx. And it was all caught on tape. Young got into it with a club employee, after he refused to give Young $8,000 in singles off his credit card. The two argued, and the employee reportedly flashed an upside-down "Hook 'Em Horns" sign, which stands for some sort of disrespect because of Vince's college.

Vince ended up with a misdemeanor citation courtesy of the Dallas Police Department. The strip club manager sued him. Three years later they settled for an undisclosed amount.

Just because an athlete is located in areas that aren't major metropolitan cities or the preferred "turn up" location, doesn't mean that they are immune to foolishness happening.

In 2006, the Indiana Pacers squad was trying to shake off the bad boy image the team earned after the infamous "Malice at the Palace" brawl. One night during preseason, teammates Stephen Jackson, Jamaal Tinsley, Marquis Daniels, and Jimmie Hunter hit up Club Rio. Something popped off inside the club; accounts say three men had a beef with Tinsley.

Jackson often describes himself as a soldier ready for war. He always has his teammates' backs. When Jackson was leaving the club, he saw drama popping off. He believed the men had the intent to shoot Tinsley.

SJack was hit in the mouth and then struck by a car going forty-five miles per hour. He then pulled out his gun and fired five warning shots. Jack ended up losing the teeth out of the front of his mouth and had to get plastic surgery to repair the damage. The

Pacers traded him to the Warriors in 2007 as part of an eight-player trade.

• • •

There are few things sadder than when an athlete doesn't know it's time to hang it up and stay out of the club.

Life post-NBA has been kind of shady at points for Steve Francis. Over the last few years, we've seen Stevie Franchise get choked up in the club by Stephen Jackson. We were dazzled as the 1999 number-two draft pick gave himself a champagne shower in a Miami club while singing Beyonce's hit "Drunk in Love." Most recently, in March of 2015, Francis was on stage with a Houston rap duo when some guy in the club snatched his chain, physically dragging him, trying to remove it. The whole incident ended up on *TMZ*.

Nightlife is a big part of the experience, and some feel it's one of the ways to continue to get that rush. But now, the promoters aren't tripping over themselves to get to him because they know he's not buying a table. Those girls that used to clamor for his attention, they've moved on to the latest hot prospect. But then, reality sets in. Seeing himself replaced both professionally and socially, no longer the Hot Athlete on the scene, can be a mind trip for a player.

Of course the easy answer is, just don't go out. But trouble can find its way into the safety of an athlete's home or hotel room.

CHAPTER 8

Computer Love

How the Internet Changed the Game for Groupies
and Athletes

Way back in 1984, Roger and Zapp sang about falling in love via a computer screen. In 2015, we are addicted to our phones and the Internet.

How an athlete navigates the lifestyle is key. But in this day, he can't hide from social media. Fans connect differently today than they did ten to fifteen years ago. Being invisible on social media will decrease marketing opportunities. There are athletes that have created whole fan movements that turned into endorsements, guest appearances, and extended shelf life, all via the Internet.

"Just don't hit send."—NFL analyst Herm Edwards

Seems like simple and practical advice. But, with the average age of both football and basketball pros being twenty-seven, these guys have never known life without the Internet or a cell phone.

The Internet has actually changed how people, especially celebs and athletes, date and socialize.

The single biggest dynamic that helped the fascination between "the life" and fan has been the Internet. Now, no matter who you are or where you're at, you have the potential to interact with your favorite jock or celebrity. That also opens up more ways to connect with the opposite sex.

Let's look at how the Internet has changed the groupie game.

In the late 1990s and early 2000s, before blogs and Twitter took over, message boards were where all the dirt poured out. There was a message board on Yahoo called "NBA Wives & Girlfriends."

That Yahoo group opened the door to creating a nationwide network of women…and eventually men—including the athletes—who wanted to keep tabs on the lifestyle.

The Yahoo group contained about two hundred members with maybe only twenty to thirty active posters. It was a mix of women who were in relationships with athletes, wives, and "jumpoffs." There were also women who stumbled into the site and were outsiders looking in. They were interested in learning the secrets to snagging a professional athlete.

Information was spilled in the group from "the Groupies' Bible." That was what the NBA Blue Book was often referred to. The book was a guide for members of the media. It contained information like; the location of the practice facility, names of the coaching, PR, and training staff. The numbers to cab companies and other useful tips when traveling to one of the other twenty-nine NBA cities.

But, more important than that for some, it contained the locations of all the visiting team hotels on the road. That info was like gold. Why compete with hundreds of girls at the club when you could just post up at the bar in the hotel lobby and "accidently" bump into an athlete or coach.

Or, for the girls who were looking to reconnect with their baller that had changed his number, she could find him at his team hotel.

The myth of the hotel lobby lined with women when team buses role in is largely false. Unless you're talking about an event like Super Bowl or All-Star.

Users shared key information about the athletes' social habits. You name it, someone on that board had experience with it and would share the details; what athlete was married but pretending he wasn't, which one had multiple girlfriends, or secret children. Where the athletes hung out after the games, partied, shopped, and dined.

Once they had the 4-1-1 down on their target, they also would coach the ladies through the best methods to get his attention, time, and/or money.

Other topics included the business side of sports, covering things like how much athletes were signing contracts for, or the difference between a guaranteed vs. nonguaranteed deal. Advice on how to break into the business side of professional sports, get a job with a team, or nurture a business relationship with an athlete. Maybe even get a bonus by adding a relationship with the job.

The first version of that group was shut down. It disappeared onc day. Word has it that one of the wives became upset with the information being spilled on her husband. So, she had the group deleted.

A new version of the group was later created, but by then, a new message board had taken over. Lipstick Alley. Only at that time, it was a message board attached to former NFL player Eddie George's fan website.

Lipstick Alley took what was happening on Yahoo and pumped it up to a level orange[6]. On Yahoo there had been a few meets ups and hookups. But it was mostly girls linking up to expand their network and have eyes in another city.

---

6 Is the highest warning alert

With Lipstick Alley, the athletes themselves got involved in the conversation. Once they discovered there was a website where women, and their friends, were discussing *all* of their business, they wanted to see what was being said and figure out who was saying it.

Bunches of your favorite blogs have probably procured information from the tea spilled on LSA. The backstory is as follows: A guy who went by the name of "the Janitor" maintained Eddie George's personal website. The message board was meant as a way for fans of Eddie's to interact with one another. Somewhere along the line, that plan went left, and it became a place where information about football players was dropped.

Eventually, the Eddie George board became a mix of sports and gossip. The block got hot for Eddie when other players began to hit him up about what posters were saying on the site. Eddie of course had no idea what was going on, and after enough complaints, he asked the Janitor to get rid of the message board.

The Janitor decided to throw an old domain on the message board, keep it and monetize it. As word continued to spread about the site, handlers got involved when several salacious topics turned up on the first page of Google searches. And then there were the lawsuits. Players, side chicks, and lots of lawyers attempted to stop the flow of information by suing the site.

The next wave happened when MySpace and Facebook took over. These became key spots for people to hook up with athletes and celebrities. Everything was in one place. You could view pictures, send private messages, and make new friends all over the country. Right from the comfort of your own home.

That of course was the prelude to Twitter. And we all know, Twitter and Instagram have been game changers.

Birdcall
Sliding in DMs like...

If you follow me on Twitter—@StilettoJill—you know that I frequently point out athlete "Birdcalls."

What's a birdcall? It's a means of communication our feathered friends use for the purpose of contact, alarm, or marking territory. It's pretty much the same thing with athletes. When your favorite athlete hits his destination and drops tweets like, "wheels up, next stop Miami," or posts a photo to Instagram with the city skyline from the plane and, "LA, what's poppin'." That is the bat signal in the sky, to alert followers that they're in the area and seeking some hijinks.

With the advancement of social media, athletes, as well as the FedEx guy, have an easier route to sex with a variety of women. I like to refer to this as "scroll and deliver." It's like takeout. Your followers are the menu items. All one needs to do is jump into the direct messages (DMs) of the one you want delivered to you.

In the nineties, groupies had to call the players at their hotel or go have drinks at the bar. If she was dialing the room, she had to hope the player of her choice wasn't staying under an alias. If he picked up, then she had be witty enough to get a conversation started. Or, just hit the jock with the truth and hope that he was flattered, thirsty, or too bored to care that she had basically stalked him.

Social media—Twitter, Instagram, Facebook, all these apps— makes it easier to skip over the awkwardness and get directly to the point. Athletes don't even have to have game or conversation to pull women.

We've seen several examples of high-profile Twitter dating; rapper Iggy Azalea and Laker Nick Young met after he made her his woman crush Wednesday.

But, when another NBA player tried that approach, things didn't run as smoothly.

Detroit Pistons player Andre Drummond decided to use "Women Crush Wednesdays" to express his huge crush on Nickelodeon *iCarly* actress Jennette McCurdy. McCurdy caught wind of Drummond's crush, which blossomed into follows on Twitter.

It quickly escalated to the gift-giving stage for Andre. The seven footer sent Jennette flowers and even a teddy bear named "Drummy." She posted a few of the gifts to Twitter. Andre took that to mean keep going, so then he stepped it up further and began sending clothing. All of this was before he ever had a face-to-face interaction with the actress.

The two hooked up in LA over a weekend to get to know each other and hang out with their friends, including Jennette's *iCarly* cast mate Nathan Kress. The weekend included laser tag, poolside activities, and a trip to Disneyland. Not bad for a first date.

But alas, all that was really just a show for Instagram. Months later, Jennette was interviewed on a podcast, where she revealed that she was never checking for Andre.

The highlights:

She said it only lasted like a week.

She wasn't attracted to him, but his repeated "Woman Crush Wednesday" posts wore her down. Plus, she was in Vegas and in a good mood when she heard about it.

She wasn't feeling him from their first text conversation. He sent his number in DM as soon as she followed him on Twitter, which she thought was a bit much. The chemistry wasn't there, but she decided to go with it for kicks and giggles.

- He'd call her on FaceTime out of the blue and be getting a massage or shopping other random things. Which was another turnoff for her.
- Her friends thought it was weird that she went out with him 'cause he wasn't her type at all. She invited all her friends on the date so it wouldn't be awkward.
- Kissing him was weird—which seems logical, since she didn't like him. That's bound to get uncomfortable.
- She was ready to break up with him after their first date, but felt bad…again, because he'd flown out to LA just to see her. So she went on more dates. He was in LA for seven days; she saw him five out of the seven.
- At one point during their first date weekend, he told her he was going out to the store to buy something. When he returned, he had a necklace. The actress claimed he dropped down on his knees in a restaurant and asked her to be his girlfriend…She wanted to say *no*, but she felt bad. But, she didn't say she turned down the jewelry.

Drummond responded that he found her comments "funny," but that he would be the mature person, accept his mistake, and keep it pushing.

While Andre's adventures in digital connections didn't go as expected, it could've ended up worse.

While the guys may be looking for easy sex, the women might be having visions of Cinderella meeting her Prince Charming via DM. The problem with easy pussy is that in reality, it isn't really easy. There's always a cost. Screenshots of conversations, penis photos, pregnancy test results, all have been leaked on social media.

You never really know who you're dealing with. It could be catfish, or it could be a stalker.

Kyrie Irving and Miss Hawaii Saga

In the summer of 2011, then number-one draft pick Kyrie Irving got his first bitter taste of life as a star in the NBA. Kyrie had to file a police report against a woman named Jessica Jackson who referred to herself on Twitter as "Miss Hawaii."

Kyrie met "Miss Hawaii" via Twitter. The two started texting, then adding in phone calls and Skype sessions. In the police report, Irving said he and Jackson met once in person, in front of the Ritz Carlton in Charleston, North Carolina, for two minutes.

Then something went wrong, Jackson started tweeting claims that Irving was harassing her to the point that she had to file a police report. Naturally she also released images of their alleged texts messages and Twitter DMs.

But it didn't stop there. Next Jackson took it to YouTube, where she talked about how she "really didn't care about Kyrie," but threatened to stab him. That's when Irving decided that it was time to put a stop to it and file a police report.

The two appeared in court where the judge had to order both of them to stop all contact with each other.

Thirst

The "social" part in social media was like opening Pandora's box. You also have to watch out for "catfishs." Catfishing is when a person creates a fake online persona in order to trick someone into a relationship. There term comes from the 2010 documentary film and MTV show of the same name.

In 2011 someone pretending to be actress Lauren London and singer Cassie, scammed several NFL and NBA players out of credit card information and plane tickets. The fakes would reach out to the athletes through bogus Twitter accounts, or through a friend of a friend. These guys never actually saw "Lauren" or "Cassie" in person, just BBM conversations, occasional phone calls, and e-mails.

The scam finally came to an end after plane tickets linking Lauren London and an athlete were leaked to the blogs. But, Lauren had no idea who the player was. Representatives got involved, a sting action was put in place that ended with Cassie and Lauren releasing a PSA to athletes and entertainers about the scam.

DM Fails

In 2009 when Twitter was still fairly new and fresh, the fifteen thousand followers of two-time NBA champion Ray Allen's account were caught off guard when hackers – or a tweet that was really meant to be a direct message by a very married Ray Allen— was sent down the timeline with heavy sexting instructions.

I'm getting there. When u masturbate think about my tongue or your clit and switching back and forth from my dick to my tongue

Yeah…

After deleting the embarrassing tweet, Allen then created a whole new Twitter account. On the old account, his last tweet was a warning about the dangers of identity theft.

On Instagram Straight Flexing

In 2015, Instagram is the top dog. Everyone is a bit wiser, having gone through some of those embarrassing moments on Twitter.

Your favorite athlete is likely cheating on you with a secret Instagram account. Why would he need a secret account? Because people are paying attention to everything and connecting the dots. Who you follow, unfollow, tag, etc.

Instagram is where it all goes down. And of course, being sexually provocative gets lots of attention. Threesomes happen, and lately it's the women that are suggesting a little "fun." The ladies recruit other willing participants through the app. I know you didn't think all those women who initiate "Women Crush Wednesday" posts were only about girl power. The setup is easy; popping bottles or smoking hookah in the club with an athlete is the bait. Times have changed; fame via Instagram is an active career trajectory for some. Groups of bad bitches win. They get attention, and it allows the ladies to shine by association. Plus the added bonus that there's something for everybody's taste pallet in a group. How does an IG starlet spend a typical day? They make their money from promotions—club promotions, weave lines, diet teas, waist shapers, etc. That requires them to shoot content daily, and by content I mean back shots and provocative poses.

I call those girls Star Panties. They're hoping to get on by association. Maybe luck up and end up on reality TV, with club hosting gigs, or in a post on JocksandStilettoJill.com—shameless plug.

If an athlete selects the right Instagram vixen, he won't need worry about how the extras are set up. He can chill while his latest conquest happily selects his new-next vixen, all from a few strategic posts.

This creates an easy opening for those women who have a desire to become a part of that scene. It usually requires being accepting of some unconventional situations.

Having sex with a smorgasbord of random bad chicks sounds like a good idea in theory, but things can quickly get out of hand.

Time Out:

One athlete got so caught up with Instagram it seemed like he developed some form of sexual ADD. This guy was injured and not on the active players roster for his team.

When he was almost set to return to play, he pretended to be injured a little longer to miss the road game targeted for his return. That's because he convinced two chicks he met on Instagram separately to all hook up. The catch was, it could only go down on that particular day. He missed his game and flew to LA for some fun. Of course they pump-faked at the last second.

• • •

We know that those who live a high-profile lifestyle are prone to get into situations that might puzzle or possibly intrigue the average person. Case in point, NBA guard Lou Williams lived every man's fantasy situation.

In 2014 Lou was rocking a nonconventional lifestyle choice of having two girlfriends. That doesn't seem too strange, but here's the twist: not only did the two know about each other, the three of them all hung out, took family trips together, and maybe more.

He even nicknamed the two "blond and brown" because of their hair color. The situation became so popular that the Toronto Raptors' global ambassador, Drake, talked about the sitchy in his song "6 Man" from his mixtape "If you're reading this, it's too late."

But soon, things took a turn. All that attention might have been the nail in the coffin. Trouble in paradise erupted after Lou allegedly flew girlfriend #2 out on the road without his main being present.

Of course there was the expected subliminal shots on social media, plus the requisite unfollowing on Instagram and deleting of photos. Over All-Star break, Lou, girlfriend #2, a few friends and teammates all went to Cabo San Lucas, Mexico. But not the main girlfriend.

The game can turn on you quickly. One minute you're the main; the next you find out Mr. Pro Athlete is openly cheating.

CHAPTER 9

Rules for Respectful Cheating

L et me state the obvious; there are a lot of women. Athletes want a sidepiece for ego points and sex. Sometimes they get caught up and fall in love, but mostly it's just for the night. Athletes *like* groupies. They like having them around; they enjoy spending time and money on them.

What's the first thing that happens at any sporting event? The anthem. It starts the game. It glorifies the freedom that comes with the position of being a citizen of the most powerful country, or in this case, a member of the top professional sports leagues in the world. It's a theme, used to convey underlying values, principles, spirit, and camaraderie. Pro athletes have anthems about women and life.

In the 2013 Showtime special, *30 Days in May*, boxing champ Floyd "Money" Mayweather Jr. compared the women in his life to cars:

"When it comes to females, even though you can't drive ten cars at one time, you got people that got ten cars," said Mayweather. "So you're able to keep maintenance up on ten cars. So I feel that as far as it comes to females, that same thing should apply. If you're able to take care of twenty, then you should have twenty."

Some of the other themes applied to handling multiple women:

"I treat them like I meet them." That means the circumstances under which a woman meets an athlete can play a role in the level of respect given.

"I treat everybody the same, even though they're all different." That means, nobody is really getting any special privileges or extended benefits.

The golden rule between athletes and women used to be "shh-hh." But, that's not the way it's working for a lot of these women today. For one, there's the lure of newfound fame that might develop as a result of putting even the most minor interaction with an athlete on blast.

Most athletes assume that women know when they're in a serious relationship. The assumption is that the women have already Googled them or follow them on social media, and that they already are aware of their situation and don't care. A favorite line athletes use to deny their very public relationship is that he and his wife are divorcing, but trying to keep that news out of the media and blogs for privacy's sake.

What Are They Really Looking For?

The classic conquest for any pro ball player, current or retired, and looking for no-strings-attached fun, is about twenty-two to twenty-five years old. If she's older, it doesn't mean she's out of the game, it just means she might have to put in some extra work.

We talked earlier how availability is key. At a moment's notice, she has to be willing to fly wherever he wants her to be, even if she ends up getting stood up once she arrives at the destination.

One superstar used to brag to teammates about his early years in the NBA. Initially, he had a girl in every city that had the NBA had a franchise. Thirty teams, in twenty-eight cities. And by girl, he wasn't saying some random he scooped up from the club if he felt like being freaky for the night. He meant a woman that believed she was in some full-blown relationship with him.

But after a couple of years, that became hard to maintain. So, he cut it down to an easier to manage fifteen. The thing to keep in mind, while he had these fifteen women in a semi-regular rotation, he still was picking up strays and engaging in the random one-nighter.

Right around his tenth year in the league, that number dropped to about four or five…plus, his wife.

He estimated that he had had sex with about one thousand women. When you think about it, in the grand scheme of things, that's ten women a year. Which you could further break down to one new conquest every two months. The way things are in 2015, with online and textual relationships, that's pretty much long-term commitment.

That number is far below the thirty thousand women that former Lakers legend Wilt Chamberlin boasted he slept with in his 1997 biography. But many have said that the number is physically impossible to reach.

When the holidays would come around, the superstar was known to send his professional friend to the mall during road trips for gifts—Louis Vuitton, Louboutin, Celine, Chanel, whatever "it" brand item was on top at that moment.

The friend would pick up a few items at different price points. Mr. Professional Athlete would then toss whatever "girlfriend" he saw during that trip a gift to keep them happy. And most importantly, *quiet*.

The number one rule to remember when cheating is so important I didn't even make it a rule. This should be a pro athlete's mantra when cheating on their significant other: no public embarrassment.

Most of the wives and girlfriends don't want to leave anyway. They know what the situation is, but they damn sure don't want to look crazy to friends and family. It's also a headache to have the entire world commenting on decisions made relating to their home below an Instagram photo of their family. The topic never comes up if the athlete does his dirt in private.

Professional golfer Tiger Woods learned that lesson the hard way. In 2009, when his multiple cheating scandals broke, his ex-wife Elin Norgin [7] hopped off the ship quickly and took a nice chunk of his money with her.

Earlier that year, evidence started popping up that Tiger was cheating on Elin with a New York club hostess. Once the news started to hit the media, Tiger's bright solution to the problem was to get his side chick to cover for him by arranging a phone conversation between her and his wife.

That made Elin even more curious about what her husband might be doing away from her. Naturally she looked to his cell phone for clues. Elin didn't try to be coy; she left messages on voice mail saying, "You know who this is because you are fucking my husband."

That's when Tiger made misstep number four, proving once again why the player life just isn't for him. He left a voice message for one of his sidepieces, asking her to put a generic outgoing message on her voice mail in case his wife called.

"Hey, it's, uh...it's Tiger," he said. "Can you please take your name off your phone? My wife went through my phone and, uh, maybe calling you. So if you can, please take your name off that. And, um....just have it as a number on the voice mail. OK? You got to do this for me. Huge. Quickly. All right, bye."

---

7 http://nypost.com/2013/11/24/the-night-tiger-woods-was-exposed-as-a-serial-cheater/

Of course the voice mail was later leaked, but that wasn't even the tip of the iceberg. Thanksgiving evening 2009 is when it all blew up.

A little after 2:00 a.m. on the Friday after Thanksgiving, one of Woods's neighbors called 9-1-1, saying the golfer had crashed his Escalade into a tree in front of his house. Tiger was taken to the hospital in "serious condition." A police chief told the Orlando Sentinel that Woods's wife Elin rescued the golf pro by breaking the rear window of the SUV with a golf club to pull him from the vehicle.

But then *TMZ* got on the case. Hours later the real story was revealed, stating that Tiger and Elin were arguing before the crash, that Elin chased him from the house with the golf club. She smashed the back of the car as Tiger was driving away. The breaking glass startled him, causing him to crash into a fire hydrant and then a tree.

Woods was rumored to have paid his club hostess $10 million to keep quiet about the scandal after she hired civil rights attorney Gloria Allred. Allred is the go-to for high-profile cases involving women and very rich men.

The rest of Tiger's harem must have heard the rumor that Tiger was giving checks to keep quiet. Soon there was an onslaught of porn stars, strippers, escorts, and party girls who said they, too, had been having sex with Tiger.

By the end December, Woods entered rehab for sex addiction. Nordegren used the time to renegotiate her prenup. She later divorced him, receiving approximately $100 million in the divorce settlement.

Woods's golf game fell apart, and his career has never fully recovered. He now earns about $54 million in endorsements—half of what he made prescandal, Forbes says—and has not won a major tournament since.

Rules to Flying Her Out:

As a pro athlete, you're going to fly someone out. It's just the rules of the game. The advice I give to my athlete friends who are cheating: don't get into a serious relationship, or if you're going to take certain risks, do it with someone that has as much to lose as you do.

But several have told me those are unreasonable suggestions. In that case, check out more tips below for successful sidepiece management:

1. Do a Hofax on your lady friend

If you hire a known thief to work in a bank, whose fault is it when they rob you? With the Internet and social media, there is absolutely no reason you can't find out vital information on the woman you are thinking about flying in.

2. Don't mess with her reality. Tell the truth

Fair exchange is no robbery. If you aren't looking for anything deep, tell her. If you already have a situation, and this is just for fun, give her a chance to say no. She might just be onboard for what you want. But you have to give her that option.

Plus, if you lie to her, she's just going to stalk your social media anyway. She will follow your wife, girlfriend, professional friends. Cousin on your stepfather's side. Whoever they can to gain intel on you and your situation, and possibly befriend your people.

Actually, that's likely to happen no matter what you do…

3. Keep your phone locked, and your money, jewelry, and wallet in the safe

She's a stranger. Keep all your valuables safe.

4. Condoms

Child support is expensive. Sucks even more if you have to issue out thousands of dollars a month to a complete stranger.

5. Consider a confidentiality agreement or cell phone ban

If this is someone you think you might want a long-term, no-strings-attached type scenario with, or you're just indulging in activities that might be potentially embarrassing if word got out, a legal agreement isn't a bad idea. In a post–Karrine "Super Head" Steffans world, where golf caddies and cousins write tell-alls about their superstar athlete relationships, enforced confidentiality agreements will become the standard.

Or, just ban cell phones at your home or hotel room so she's not sneaking flicks for the "just in case" file.

5a. If you opt for a long-term temporary scenario, make sure you have a designated professional friend to deal with her if things go left and you need to drop all contact.

6. "Booking info" sometimes means she has a price

You know how you'll look at a half-naked girl's Instagram page, and she'll have booking contact info? Don't be surprised if that date with the "model" comes with a price tag. The Internet has birthed a number of entrepreneurial enterprises, escorting being among them. Some of these women have a fee…A lot of athletes are OK with it.

One popular reality TV star gets paid $10,000 just to go on a first date. No sex, you're just paying for her company and to be seen with her.

7. If you're making payments, be on time

Don't get caught up thinking these chicks love you. If you make a woman disposable, she will think the same about you. They want to get what they can before you discard them. Therefore, if you make a promise, pay up!

In 2006, former New York Knicks star Stephon Marbury agreed to pay his former chef/part-time lover, Thurayyah Mitchell, $1 million in hush money to keep the details of their affair quiet. Marbury was married at the time with three children. Initially Mitchell threatened to file a sexual harassment suit, stating that Marbury made her feel sex with him was part of the job.

Eventually they reached a million-dollar settlement. Mitchell sued Marbury when he stopped making payments after dishing out $600K. Steph ended up having to pay the money anyway, and everyone ended up finding out details of the situation when *TMZ* reported the news of the lawsuit. The lesson here is, keep your sidepieces paid on time to retain their silence.

8. Know where you're keeping the B phone

Tiger Woods could've avoided a lot of his problems by just having a secret phone that he kept in the car or the bottom of his golf bag.

So now you're cheating. You have a great rotation of wifey, side chick, fun girls, and randoms. You're living the life. But there is a flip side to all of this that you better prepare yourself for.

9. Wifey is going to cheat.

Former NBA player Winston Bennett was a midlevel player who managed to sleep with around ninety women a month—even while married— he even brought home two STDs to his wife during his playing days. When asked in an interview would he stay if he found out his wife was cheating, Bennett's response was, "absolutely not."

Sounds good, but it's foolish to think that while you're doing all that dirt in the streets with random women, your significant other is going to stay loyal. Everyone gets tired, and lonely. It could be a teammate's shoulder she cries on about all your dirty deeds.

Think about the "friendship" between Spurs' guard Tony Parker and his former teammate Brent Barry's wife[8] Erin. At the time, Tony was married to actress Eva Longoria. The two couples were friends. Eva reportedly discovered text—and sext—messages between Tony and Erin that sealed the deal for her to file for divorce. Brent and Erin were already going through a divorce after twelve years of marriage; Eva and Tony divorced after only three years.

• • •

A random one-off with a "hot" waitress or a club chick is one thing. But a full-blown relationship where there's an emotional attachment will always hurt more. Sleeping with *any* of these women without protecting yourself—and by extension, your wife—is a setup for drama.

Revealing *any* details about your home life to these other women will likely leave your mate embarrassed, hurt, and ashamed. There's nothing like hearing the details of your life from the woman sleeping with your man.

Bottom line, if you're going to indulge in those side situations, understand that every time you go back to chick 2B, you're adding to the amount your main chick is going to charge you for her heartache when all the nasty details come out. Because, in all likelihood, the tea will pour.

---

8 http://www.nydailynews.com/entertainment/gossip/erin-barry-tony-parker-sexting-relationship-physical-reports-article-1.452204

CHAPTER 10

Athletes Are Groupies, Too

O nce the jock has conquered the baddest chicks in the city and run through all his hometown throwback pussy, the ambitious jock is looking to take his collection of "work" to the next level.

As an athlete, once you start feeling your swag, it's time to step your cookies up. What used to seem top-notch now becomes passé. You begin to transcend your surroundings. You've seen more, and now you want to conquer more.

What comes with this ascension to the next level? An upgrade of course. At this point, it's safe to assume that the professional athlete has got a couple of Internet starlets under his belt. To you the star panty might be overexposed, and surgically enhanced. But to many, she is a status symbol.

The crown jewel to the professional athlete kit is a bad chick. And, the epitome of a bad chick is a celebrity.

What says "salute me, muthafuckas" more than having a celebrity chick on your arm? Probably a championship ring, but a celebrity chick might be easier to obtain than a ring for some of these athletes.

So, why shoot for a celebrity chick? Status matters. A reality TV star, singer, or actress is ranked as a higher priority than your garden-variety nurse or teacher. Because in theory, she's rare—not just anybody can get one, and it helps their legend grow. Everyone wants to be a power couple. They want a woman who can be the Beyonce to his Jay Z. Plus, she can relate to his complicated work-life mix because her career is crazy, too.

People are quick to label women groupies, but athletes are groupies, too. The idea of "booing" up with that star from his top-five all-time list back in college does something amazing to the psyche.

In reality, it's the other side of the coin to some groupie's pursuit of the jocks.

Some athletes excel at this pursuit, mastering the balancing act of getting just the right amount of press and props from the public.

Lessons from Derek Jeter

Not everyone can move through the life like former Yankees' star Derek Jeter. "The Captain" was the king of the high-profile relationship during his nineteen-year career in professional baseball.

Jeter has been linked to more bad chicks than NBA players are to reality starlets and Instagram models. The list includes[9] pop star Mariah Carey, Actress Minka Kelly, former Miss Universe Lara Dutta, Victoria's Secret model Adriana Lima, actresses Jessica Alba, Jessica Biel, Jordana Brewster, and Vanessa Minnillo. Some of the rumored hookups include supermodel Tyra Banks, Gabrielle Union and actress Scarlett Johannson.

Jeter also knows how to treat the ladies. Per a 2011 *New York Post* article, Jeter made sure to send the ladies on their way after an overnight stay in a car service. Plus he'd arrange for a postdate gift basket

---

9 http://www.ibtimes.com/derek-jeter-girlfriends-who-has-yankees-star-dated-photos-1555422

with various Jeter memorabilia as a takeaway. Add in the fact that Jeter retired with zero baby mamas, I'd say he mastered the formula.

Perhaps it was the rumored institution of a no cell phone policy coupled with the use of confidentiality agreements.

Jeter reportedly has a strict no camera/cell phone policy in his home. A lot of athletes and entertainers have a similar mandate. Some have confidentiality contracts that include photos, copies of government issued IDs, and your signature. The agreements also include clause for tweeting or Instagraming activities inside of the home.

Others don't fair the waters so smoothly and end up playing themselves.

Time Out:
Play #2: Triangle offense—the rapper,
the ball player, & the R&B chick

On the court E3 was known for being talented but a bit out of control. Off the court he was a bit of a knucklehead yet extremely charming when it came to the ladies. He gave a lot of attention and good gifts. He seemed to enjoy buying presents for all the women he dated, even in the most casual use of the term "dating." He fell in love *quick*. And out of it even faster.

When E3 got chance to get next to this semi-popular "songstress," he couldn't wait to overwhelm her with his game.

The songstress was close to a superstar singer. The superstar singer was involved with a popular rapper. E3 saw the connections lighting up.

He wanted to get in with that crowd and establish himself on another level. The problem was, E3 was way too comfortable in the situation with the songstress, but she wasn't quite into him yet. She did however accept his gifts and played along. Why not?

NBA All-Star Weekend was coming up, that takes place in February, and it's usually pretty close to Valentine's Day. E3 wanted to show out and let everybody know who his girl was. Plus, let her know she was "wifey." He went shopping for a fur and diamond earrings. Mind you, they haven't had sex yet. At this point, they haven't even shared a really good hug.

When E3 arrived at All-Star weekend, he immediately began hitting the songstress's phone. Dude blew her up. She finally let him come visit her for a minute at her hotel. E3 was pressing her to link up later, he wanted her whole night; dinner, a party, and of course back to his room later.

The songstress told him that she was probably going to stay the night with her BFF superstar friend.

E3 was pressed; he decided that he wanted to be at her room, just in case she changed her mind. He saw her spare hotel room key on the table and slipped it into his pocket when she wasn't paying attention. His plan was to surprise her later and set up the room.

The night goes on. E3 parties, separate from the songstress, but of course, she's his real focus for the night. After he leaves his function, he once again starts texting his boo, thinking he'll be able to talk her into spending the night with him. She's responding, but it's clear she's not trying to see him.

E3 decides he's just going to take control of the situation and go wait in her room...without telling her! He gets to her hotel, walks into the room, thinking he's about to post up, chill, and get that pussy.

Surprise #1, he walks in and finds her homegirl there—she's a singer/actress, too— she was shocked to see E3. She was expecting room service.

But that's not a problem. The room was a suite. He just thinks the singer/actress is going to be listening to her friend getting the dick for the rest of the night.

E3 continues through the suite to the bedroom.

When he walks into the bedroom, he gets surprise #2. A popular Rap Star is posted up, chilling with the songstress.

Nobody says a word. The Rapper finally laughs. The songstress is *shook*! She looks at E3 and asks him what was he doing there. E3 walks into the room, gives the rapper a pound—he's a fan of his work—and takes a seat in a chair.

The Rapper knew the songstress was "dating" E3. He also knew she wasn't feeling him, so he was amused by all of E3's antics.

The rapper decided to say his good-byes and leave. The songstress is still in shock that this actually went down and asks E3 to leave, too. Now E3's upset the rest of the night because his boo, was boo'd up with a rapper. The songstress was sick, too…about the rapper catching her. That's who really had her heart.

But, there was a happy ending to all of this. E3 was really a superfan of the Rapper. So much so in fact, he later got the name of the rapper's crew tatted on him.

• • •

The Kardashian Effect—Reality TV

Christina Milian's character Paris in *Love Don't Cost a Thing* said, "Popularity is a job. Work to get it, work to keep it." That's so true, especially in this social media–driven world we live in. Social currency matters, and some guys are willing to go the extra mile to gain relevance there.

If you really think about, MTV is to blame for athletes and reality show stars merging. It started back in the early nineties with the original *Real World*. In season one, one of the roommates, an aspiring rapper named Heather B, had a crush on former NBAer Larry Johnson. Heather got the opportunity to meet him on the show as a featured storyline.

During the height of the Lakers' back-to-back titles in 2010 and 2011, Lamar Odom was featured all over TV. He was playing for the World Champs, seen weekly on the hit E! reality show, *Keeping Up with the Kardashians*, and the only other Laker outside of Kobe to have national commercials. Kobe wasn't actually *in* his commercial spot; he was featured as a puppet along with a puppet-version of LeBron James.

During this time frame, Lamar had endorsement deals with Taco Bell, Power Bar, Samsung, and his own unisex cologne named "Unbreakable" with wife, Khloe. Lamar was a key piece to those Lakers teams, but the commercial boost was definitely from his association with the Kardashian family.

For a time, being on a reality show was a highly coveted goal for athletes. Some of the names of pro athletes that have been featured on reality TV over the last fifteen years include Carmelo Anthony (NBA), Matt Barnes (NBA), Terrell Owens (NFL), Chad "Ochocinco" Johnson (NFL), Eric Decker (NFL), Ndamukong Suh (NFL), Kris Humphries (NBA), Reggie Bush (NFL), Jesse Palmer (NFL), Jose Canseco (retired MLB), Kordell Stewart (retired NFL), ex-NFL star and current analyst, Deion Sanders, NBA owner Mark Cuban, and the granddaddy of athletes and reality TV, Shaq.

Shaq has participated as a guest, host, or subject of at least ten reality shows. From the moment Shaq began his NBA career in 1992, he was involved in the entertainment business, starring in films, and putting out albums. His ex-wife Shaunie had experience in entertainment also, at one point working as an administrative assistant for a TV and film studio. Shaq was one of the first athletes to jump on the reality TV wave early with a 2005 docu-series on ESPN that ran for six episodes, before each game of the 2005 Western Conference Finals and before Game One of the NBA Finals that year.

Shaunie parlayed her experience with Shaq and reality TV into VH1's Basketball Wives franchise, which included five seasons of the original *Miami* show, plus three spin-off shows: *Football Wives* which featured NFL Hall of Famer Deion Sanders's then-wife Pilar, *Baseball Wives*, and *Basketball Wives LA*.

A fifth show was planned for Shaunie and her kids, but Shaq took Shaunie to court to block their children appearing on a reality show for VH1, claiming there was too much pressure from producers to create a wholesome show. Shaunie countered with claims Shaq simply didn't want the world to know he was an absent dad.

The original Basketball Wives franchise causes quite a bit of controversy. Early plans for the cast, centered on wives and girlfriends connected to the Miami Heat where Shaq won his fourth NBA Championship. If you ever watched the hit VH1 show, the names of the teams associated with the cast members were never mentioned. Only the cities associated with the teams. That's because the NBA wanted it clear that it had no connection to the show.

It was also rumored that Heat GM Pat Riley put the hammer down on any member of the Heat or their significant other thinking about appearing on the production. Shaunie later said the reason why more wives of active players didn't appear on the show was because the athletes feared messy sidepieces starting drama out of jealousy.

Several lawsuits were filed by NBA players against the show. Dwight Howard, Gilbert Arenas, and Chris Bosh all filed legal action to prevent their name or "personal business" from ending up on VH1.

People tend to think that every single situation on reality TV is a setup. That there is a script for the cast to memorize, and all the arguments or "situations" are fake. While there's absolutely a bit of theatrical exaggeration and fiction sprinkled in, real life situations come to life from those "story lines."

One of the early developments on VH1's reality show *Basketball Wives* centered on Shaunie's belief that Laura Govan, the sister of Shaunie's cast member Gloria, had an affair with Shaq while he and Shaunie were still married.

When we were first introduced to Gloria Govan—the estranged wife of NBA forward Matt Barnes—she and Matt were new parents, and newly engaged. Gloria was considered the "naive" one, even calling her castmates bitter and jealous. Matt and Gloria maintained that season one was a terrible experience and they wouldn't be returning for season two. But their storyline was too juicy and the allure of the bright lights was too much to ignore.

Although the couple ended up calling off their wedding between seasons one and two, alerting their friends via text message, the couple came back and moved on to the spin-off show in LA; the attention factor of reality TV can be addictive.

Gloria and Matt once again separated, but hid that fact from producers of the show. One of the byproducts of that experience, were allegations that Gloria's newfound fame had caused her to spread her love around to industry men. Matt had a very public Twitter beef with rapper the Game and his associate over Gloria that was pretty nasty.

Once again, the two reconciled and eloped away from the cameras, pissing of the producers. More beefs and physical altercations erupted with the LA cast, and after two seasons, Gloria and her sister Laura left the show.

Fast forward to 2014, Matt and Gloria became estranged once again and are headed for divorce. Matt would later say that being on reality TV hurt his relationship with his wife, and that teams didn't really want their players participating in those type of shows.

But back to that Kardashian effect, it's great when it's working. While dating a Kardashain, Reggie Bush won the Super Bowl with the New Orleans Saints, Kris Humphries became the NBA's Most Improved Player, and Lamar Odom won Sixth Man of the Year honors. Granted, we also know all those situations crashed and burned a short time after, but you get the idea.

Even the son of Mike Brown – former Lakers head coach - was hoping to catch on the Kardashian wave. He wanted his dad to introduce him to Lamar because his plan was to have him hook up an introduction with one of the Kardashians' younger teenage Jenner sisters.

Reality TV gave athletes another area to gain relevance. The extra check was nice, but building an audience outside sports was the real sweet spot. Unless of course you're an athlete that's already gone broke. Then the double dose of income and attention are probably equal.

Time Out:
Play #3—The reality star, the R&B singer, & the athlete
Raya—a popular reality star—is not the type of women who is going to wait her turn. She knows what she wants, and she also knows
what she wants from you. *If* you have something she can capitalize
on, then she'll deal with you. For her, it breaks down to assets and
liabilities. You're either one or the other.

Raya was already dating a very married veteran player. But, she
wasn't putting all her eggs in one basket. No matter what they say,
they aren't leaving the wife. So, getting some sort of tangible benefit
from the situation is a must.

By tangible Raya meant funds, gifts, and investments for her
future. Raya had started to date an R&B singer who had recently
stepped into film. Although he was tight as hell with his cash, the
benefit of him was that he had a few film projects coming up. Raya
knew there would be a role in there for her. Again, it's about benefits.

One night Raya and the singer were chilling at her house. The
house that her married basketball veteran was currently paying the
mortgage on.

Raya and singer hadn't started the sexual relationship yet, but
this cozy evening at home was the perfect way for it to pop off. The
vet had been texting Raya all evening. She had been MIA on the vet
since she started trying to secure her spot with the singer.

About halfway through the first movie, Raya and the singer were
boo'd up on the couch, enjoying each other's company, when in
walked the vet, demanding to know why Raya was playing games.
He came in through her garage and knew her gate code.

The R&B singer wasn't about that life. While Raya and the vet
went at it arguing, the singer sneaked out of the house, preventing a
TMZ scandal in the process.

Favorite Athlete-Celebrity Couple

- Carmelo Anthony and Lala Vasquez-Anthony
- David Beckham and Victoria Beckham
- Gabrielle Union and Dwyane Wade
- Tom Brady and Giselle Bundchen
- Kerry Washington and Nnamdi Asomugha—they managed to keep their entire relationship out of the public eye
- Serge Ibaka and Keri Hilson

Throwbacks

- Rodney Peete and Holly Robinson-Peete
- Jason Sehorn and Angie Harmon—the couple broke up in 2014 after thirteen years of marriage
- Khloe Kardashian and Lamar Odom—I liked them together; I thought they were gonna make it
- Kim Kardashian and Reggie Bush
- Matt Kemp and Rihanna
- The ultimate throwback athlete-celebrity pairing, Yankees Joe DiMaggio and every groupie's favorite golden girl, Marilyn Monroe

CHAPTER 11

Wifey

Good girl with a heart of gold or fun girl with finance on her mind, the goal is usually the same. To get a ring and become Mrs. Professional Athlete. Just like with athletes, a ring is important. A lot of status and perks come with the title. It also makes the athlete appear more stable to the public eye.

People will always ask if the significant other of an athlete met him before he got into the league—like a high school or college sweetheart—or after he was drafted. The answer to that question tends to determine whether or not they believe the wife is there for the man or the money.

The perks: fame by association, socializing with celebs, and of course, access to the money. But everything has its price. Infidelity clouds many of these situations. Relationships with jocks come with a few rules of engagement. A girl has two choices: adapt or get used to hurt feelings.

The number one question, do the wives and wifeys know what goes on with the "randoms"? *Yes*, a lot of the time they know their men have strayed from the relationship.

The reasons they stay in the relationships are varied. Some really love the man behind the "Mr. Professional Athlete" persona. They try to work through their issues. Others don't want to break up their family, so they turn a blind eye to the foolishness. And then there are those who are addicted to the lifestyle and perks. In some cases it's a combination of all three.

With the rise in popularity of reality shows about "wives," especially those that are connected to sports figures, the fascination with their lifestyle has reached extreme levels.

Are they really shopping all day, just to post their designer purchases to Instagram? How can these women maintain their self-respect knowing he's out getting caught up with random women, hanging at the club, or taking the Memorial Day weekend trek to Vegas?

That's why you have to commend the women who get involved and manage to turn heartbreak and scandal into something beneficial. I present to you the Professional Athlete Wifey Mt. Rushmore. These are the women that groupies and gold diggers everywhere idolize, and whose lifestyles they're trying to emulate and obtain. Because in a game that few women really win at, these women came out on top.

Professional Athlete Wifey Mt. Rushmore

"Living like Givens scheming on Tyson."—Kool Moe Dee

Robin Givens:
You have to include Robin Givens in the mix because her relationship with Mike Tyson was a game changer. 23-year old Givens married the 21-year-old boxing champ in 1988, just eleven months after meeting him. Back in the eighties, Robin was one of the stars of the hit ABC sitcom *Head of the Class*. She was one of the "It Girls" at the time.

The story of Robin hooking up with a street kid like Tyson was huge. A former Sarah Lawrence student turned Hollywood actress marring a brute like Iron Mike raised a few eyebrows.

Before Robin met Mike, she dated another high profile sports' figure also named Mike. Michael Jordan was rising in popularity at the time when the two met. Robin also dated one of the eighties biggest stars, actor-comedian Eddie Murphy. Robin and Tyson met at the height of his boxing career in 1987. At the time the legendary fighter was worth $50 million.

If you go by Tyson's version of events in his 2013 memoir, *Undisputed*, Robin and her mother, Ruth Roper, were the undisputed champions of scheming and plotting to get a young, naive athlete's millions. He said they added to that mix by using the media to humiliate him while attempting to exploit him. Givens was three months pregnant at the time of the wedding. There was no prenup.

Soon after the wedding, Tyson says Givens and Roper went shopping for a mansion. They found one in a New Jersey suburb for $5 million. According to Tyson, he paid the entire $5 million upfront. Robyn had a miscarriage shortly after they moved into their new home.

Gold Diggin' Has Its Face

Their appearance as a couple on ABC's *20/20* with Barbara Walters forever changed sports fans feelings about Robin Givens and her upgrade of the champ.

With Mike next to her, looking as if he were in some sort of drug-induced haze, Givens told Walters how much she and her mom loved Mike, but that they were terrified of him at times because he was such an animal. She described living with him as hell, and indicated that he was physically abusive.

Shortly after, Givens filed for divorce, after only eight months of marriage. Per Tyson, she also asked for *half* of his millions. He later said he felt setup, that Robin and her mother attempted to separate him from his friends and humiliate him on national TV.

Pop culture took the appearance hard. Robin's name was even dropped into hip-hop lyrics back in the day. Eighties rapper Kool Moe Dee spit the line, "Living like Givens scheming on Tyson." Rap group EPMD started a whole anti–gold digger movement with their song "Gold Digger," that was reportedly inspired by Givens and Tyson.

Years later while Tyson was on a talk show, he shared a story about how he and Robin were still hooking up and having sex while going through their divorce. He said in his eyes, he was still paying for things, so that entitled him to some pussy from Givens every now and then.

One afternoon in particular, Tyson showed up at Givens's home. She wasn't there, so he waited for her to arrive. When Robin showed up, she had her new boyfriend in the passenger seat, actor Brad Pitt. [10] That was absolutely a blow to his ego.

Robin reportedly received $10 million in the divorce settlement. She claims she didn't receive anything. Tyson earned $300 million throughout his boxing career, but lost all of it spending it on extravagances like mansions, luxury cars, and pet tigers.

Juanita Jordan

Juanita Vanoy snagged the most eligible bachelor in the NBA back in the eighties. Before dating MJ, the former model and executive assistant at the American Bar Association, was rumored to have

---

10 http://abcnews.go.com/blogs/entertainment/2012/12/mike-tyson-on-catching-brad-pitt-with-his-ex-robin-givens/

briefly dated Jordan's teammate Reggie Theus. Jordan wasn't fond of Theus, he was traded from Chicago right before their championship run. In fact, in 1991 there were talks of a trade that would've returned Theus to the Bulls, but Jordan reportedly informed Bulls brass he'd quit if that happened.

Jordan and Juanita first met at Bennigan's restaurant in Chicago in March of 1985 after she attended a Bulls game. Jordan was twenty-six at the time and Juanita was thirty.

Juanita became pregnant with Jordan's first child in 1988. She reportedly spent almost a year debating if she should file a paternity suit[11]. Instead she and Jordan got married at 3:30 a.m. on September 2, 1989, at the Little White Chapel in Las Vegas while wearing jeans. Their oldest son Jeffrey was ten months old at the time. MJ married Juanita with no prenup. But don't trip; Jordan had a postnup created a year and a half after the wedding.

Rumors of infidelity popped up over their seventeen-year marriage, but Juanita has remained silent about the details. Two years into his marriage, Jordan was already allegedly paying $250K in hush money to a mistress named Karla Knafel.

MJ and Juanita have three children together, sons Jeffrey and Marcus, and daughter, Jasmine. Jordan and Juanita originally filed for divorce in January 2002, citing irreconcilable differences, but reconciled shortly thereafter. The couple reportedly tried marriage counseling but filed again for divorce in 2006.

Over the course of their relationship, MJ became the biggest star in basketball, winning six NBA titles and creating the billion-dollar Jordan brand with Nike. By the time the marriage ended, Jordan was worth $500 million. Juanita reportedly received a $168 million settlement, making their divorce the largest celebrity settlement on

---

11 http://www.people.com/people/archive/article/0,,20136227,00.html

public record at the time. Of course he's a billionaire now and on to marriage number two, but I'm sure there was a gag order attached to a settlement that large.

"Give you ice like Kobe's wife...I can make you a celebrity overnight."—Twista feat+uring Kanye West

Vanessa Bryant

Vanessa Bryant was probably the most controversial of the bunch. Vanessa was a seventeen-year-old high school senior when she and the twenty-one-year-old Lakers superstar Kobe Bryant met on set at a 1999 music video shoot. Kobe went hard in the paint to romance Vanessa. He would send her dozens of roses to her high school and made sure to be there when the final bell sounded, picking her up in his Benz after school. It reached a point that school officials finally said Kobe was causing too much of a disturbance, so Vanessa finished her senior year through home school.

Six months later, the couple was engaged. Vanessa's engagement ring was seven carats and worth $100,000. Who can forget the first image of Vanessa at the Lakers game with her huge rock, long acrylic nails, dark lip liner, streaked blonde hair and a leopard-print bucket hat?

Kobe reportedly alienated his family with his relationship with Vanessa. The two married in April 2001, with less than a dozen people in attendance. Kobe's parents, sisters, teammates, and agent, Arn Tellem, did not attend. You know what else was missing? A prenup.

But who needs one when your man is making appearances on shows like MTV's *Diary*, flashing his wedding ring, telling women to back off.

Alas, the Bryants' marriage was shaken up after Kobe admitted to infidelity in the summer of 2003. The Lakers star was charged with sexually assaulting a woman in Colorado. Kobe insisted the sex was consensual. The nineteen-year-old who accused Kobe of assault decided not to testify in September 2004, after filing a civil suit against Bryant. The charges against Kobe were eventually dropped.

Vanessa Bryant stood by her man throughout the proceedings, saying that the only thing he was guilty of was "the mistake of adultery."

Kobe bought Vanessa the infamous eight-carat, four-million-dollar, purple diamond makeup ring. Though many assumed it was directly tied to the charges, there were reports he actually ordered the ring two weeks before the incident. He also invested in his first ugly tattoo, naturally dedicated to his queen, Vanessa.

In 2005, Vanessa suffered an ectopic pregnancy and miscarried. In his Showtime documentary, *Kobe Bryant's Muse*, the seventeen-time NBA All-Star said he felt the stress of the Colorado situation caused Vanessa to have a miscarriage. Kobe dropped $50,000 on a recommitment ceremony to Vanessa that same year.

Still, in December 2011, Vanessa decided to pull the plug on her decade-long marriage to the five-time NBA champion. She filed for divorce, citing the generic "irreconcilable differences." She asked that the couple have joint custody of their two young daughters.

Drake even dropped a lyric about Vanessa taking half of Kobe's dollars in Rick Ross's "Stay Scheming."

*"Kobe 'bout to lose a hundred fifty Ms / Kobe my n***a I hate it had to be him / B**ch, you wasn't with me shooting in the gym / (B**ch, you wasn't with me shooting in the gym.)"*

With no prenuptial agreement in place, and Kobe's estimated worth at the time around $150 million, Vanessa was expected to get half, which included keeping all the jewelry he gifted her with and three mansions he signed over to her while they were separated, worth approximately $18 million.

The couple later reconciled and canceled the divorce petition. Vanessa even got to keep the homes in her name.

Evelyn Lozada

Reality TV star Evelyn Lozada executed the trifecta, becoming a three-sport all-star. She first dated basketball star Antoine Walker, later walked down the aisle with NFL wide receiver Chad "Ochocinco" Johnson, and most recently, became engaged to baseball outfielder Carl Crawford.

Evelyn met fourteen-year NBA veteran Antoine Walker in 1999 in New York at Club Envy while working for an entertainment attorney. The two exchanged numbers, and Walker invited Evelyn to a game the next day, but she turned him down. Two weeks later Walker hit Evelyn at three in the morning, and the two ended up talking for three hours. After that the two were inseparable, spending the summer together, including a vacation in Cancun, Mexico.

Initially Evelyn would travel back and forth to see Antoine while he played for the Boston Celtics, Dallas Mavericks, and Atlanta Hawks. She eventually made the decision to quit her job, uproot her daughter Shanice, and move in with Antoine. The two became engaged in 2007 while Antoine was with the Miami Heat.

Antoine, a three-time all-star, lost his $110 million fortune, and was forced to declare bankruptcy in 2010, just two years after retiring from the NBA. Antoine claims he spent millions on Evelyn during their ten-year relationship, but feels Evelyn left him when things got rough.

In a 2014 interview, Antoine said that with all Evelyn's success, she never offered to help him out financially when he hit his rough patch. Antoine felt that after looking out for her daughter and family, this was the least she could do.

Evelyn on the other hand said relationship was over for at least two years before the official breakup. She also confirmed that Antoine cheated numerous times during their relationship. Evelyn made the decision to leave the relationship because she didn't want to expose her then teenaged daughter to that negative environment any longer.

Evelyn broke up with Antoine and sold her engagement ring to fund a shoe store in Miami with another friend who had also been involved with an NBA player. Then in 2010 she starred in VH1's breakout hit reality show *Basketball Wives*.

Chad Johnson and Evelyn met on Twitter while VH1 was airing season one of the hit show. The cast attended a Super Bowl party Chad threw in 2010 that was featured on an episode. The two ended up in a battle over Twitter because Ev said the party was just OK, and it wasn't really at his house. Johnson's approximated net worth at the time, $56 million.

It was a match made in reality TV heaven. The romance started as Ochocinco was filming his own reality dating show for VH1, taking over where Flavor Flav, Brett Michaels, and Ray J failed. The finale of that show was anti-climactic, since most of the audience knew that Chad and Evelyn were already in full swing.

Somewhere along the lines, the situation blossomed into love. The couple went on their first date in front of the cameras, after months of Skyping and talking on the phone. The season-two finale of *Basketball Wives* featured Chad and Evelyn showing us that sex on the first date can lead to marriage.

As their relationship played out over seasons two, three, and four, the couple openly discussed things topics like threesomes being on the table for the relationship and cheating sscenarios while cameras rolled. The two eventually scored a wedding spin-off special, after Chad proposed with a ten-carat ring while playing the video game "Call of Duty."

But it all came crashing down in 2012. Forty-two days after the couple exchanged 4th of July I do's, in an island ceremony for cameras, Evelyn filed for divorce. The couple had an altercation that resulted in Chad's arrest for domestic violence, and subsequently saw him dropped from the Dolphins, and VH1canceling their wedding special spin-off.

While unloading groceries, Evelyn found a receipt for condoms with a purchase date not long after they were married. Evelyn said she confronted Chad and said he flew into a rage that ended in a head butt.

Next up is Dodgers outfielder Carl Crawford. The two met in 2013, and Lozada says he saved her life. I know you're wondering about Crawford's contract when the couple met. In 2010 Crawford signed a seven-year, $142 million deal. The upgrade in full effect.

Crawford proposed to Evelyn in 2014, shortly before the birth of their son Carl Leo. Naturally the engagement ring topped the previous two. Carl presented Evelyn with a fourteen-carat, $1.4 million stunner.

Robin represented the awakening, Juanita Jordan the goal, Vanessa Bryant showed you how a purple diamond and an ugly tattoo can take the sting of public humiliation away, and Evelyn Lozada taught you what bounce back looks like in motion.

But not everyone ends up a winner.

These are the seven things to remember when embarking on a serious relationship with a professional athlete:

He's going to cheat

The number one rule to remember: athletes aren't going to be faithful. If you aren't ready for that truth, this probably isn't the lifestyle for you. It doesn't mean that they will be cheating on you for the entire relationship, but the likelihood that he will step out on the relationship is *high*.

The positive is that if you're into gifts, this is usually the time when you can get one of those big-ticket items you've had your eye on. One fiancée would get a new purse or an expensive piece of jewelry whenever she caught Mr. Professional Athlete cheating. Those type of "I'm sorry" bauaubles are often referred to as "painkillers." They provide a temporary fix for the sting of infidelity. Whether it's a new car, shoes, or plastic surgery, gifts are used to ease the pain of frequent cheating.

In a lot of the recent scandals involving cheating athletes and break babies, the woman received her engagement ring after news broke that the athlete had fathered a child outside his relationship.

A cheat ring is one that's given as a makeup gift to apologize for a big public fuckup. This ring should not be confused with the "shut up" ring. That one is given to make a woman think she's on the path to marriage, but it's really just to keep her content for the moment.

It's rarely about you

That's not to say that athletes are always selfish. Nor is it to imply that they don't love their significant others, but being a pro athlete requires more effort than the usual nine-to-five in theory. There can be heavy demands on his time, exposure to tons of brown nosers, and he's bringing in the big bucks. It's a relationship that requires a lot of flexibility, and generally it's the girlfriend or wife that has to be the most elastic.

Trust is required

Trust is an important factor with any relationship. But when you're dealing with someone in the limelight. Someone who will have a lot of interaction with women, you have to find security in whatever situation you've built.

It takes a strong woman to handle some of the situations a pro athlete finds himself in. There's also that added layer of public scrutiny you'll face because you are celebrity adjacent by dating a professional athlete.

Learn his sport if you aren't familiar

Pretty self-explanatory. Be his biggest cheerleader.

Go on the road with him sometimes

Nobody's saying you have to turn into OG Jackie Christie. Back in the day, Jackie had a reputation as an NBA wife determined to keep her husband Doug faithful and away from temptation. Throughout the years, many of Jackie's extreme methods have been documented, including not allowing female reporters to interview Doug, and attending every road game—that's forty-one games. The couple had two young children who Jackie's mother cared for while she was on the road with Doug.

Jackie would drive behind the team bus while Doug was on his way to the arena, talking to him on his cell to ensure he didn't have time to have conversations with other women.

That's a bit extreme. I'm just suggesting spending some quality time with your boo while he's on the road. It allows the two of you to reconnect in a different space and gives him less free time, too wander off.

A word of warning: there will be a time you'll have to make the decision whether to turn a blind eye to the activities of his teammates' indiscretions. There are unspoken rules to the road. There could be a time when you'll have to choose between your friendship with his wife, who you sit next to at every home game, and his cool-ass sidepiece who you ran into shopping while on the road.

On the positive side, there's the added bonus that you and the other ladies can be each other's eyes and ears when you can't be around. Be sure to make those moves strategically, many teammate disagreements have started because of information shared between wives and girlfriends about a player's habits.

Just like there are player hierarchies within teams, there's one for the significant others, too. Wives come first—superstar's wives and girlfriends automatically leapfrog to the front, with visiting or long distance girlfriends shuffled toward the bottom. Remember most of these ladies aren't truly your friends. You probably won't hear from them if your significant other is traded or cut. Proceed with caution.

Find something to do with your time

Look, driving around in Bentleys, shopping, hitting the gym or spa whenever you feel like it is great, but that gets boring too. If you don't have something to put your energy into, you'll find yourself lurking in places you shouldn't be. There's a lot of loneliness attached to this lifestyle.

If your whole life revolves around Mr. Professional Athlete, it's easy to get lost in the process. Also, if he is your only source of income, make sure you start a "just in case" slush fund. At any given moment, he can say, "I'm cutting your credit card." Then what happens?

It's hard to keep a regular job if you're living with your pro athlete. Chances are you'll be living in at least two different cities per year, and with trades, you never know where you might end up. Start a charity, create an Instagram boutique, find something to do with idle time.

Plan for divorce

Everyone wants to believe in happily ever after. But the numbers are telling a specific story. Sixty to eighty percent of athletes end up divorcing following retirement[12]. Break babies and shut-up rings lead to bad marriages and strained relationships, with infidelity and financial issues being the most prevalent causes for divorce among pro athletes.

Always get a prenup. Yes, I understand that it's about love. No one in love is getting married to get a divorce. But statistically speaking, this love won't last. Therefore, it's in everyone's best interest to cover the basics. As a professional athlete, you should know that you're going to have to come out of pocket if you divorce. Consider it a cost of doing business.

Sometimes it *is* cheaper to keep her. I'm not advocating staying in a bad marriage. But divorce can be costly. NBA superstar Dwyane Wade married his high school sweetheart Siohvaughn Funches while in college. DWade was drafted fourth in the 2003 NBA draft to the Miami Heat.

The following summer, Shaq was traded to Miami, along with all the turn up that comes along when the Big Diesel steps on the scene. Wade morphed into Flash, and the Heat won an NBA title in '06.

---

12   http://www.nytimes.com/2009/08/09/sports/football/09marriage.html

But by 2007, with infidelity accusations coming from both sides, Miami had worn the Wades' marriage down. Siohvaughn filed for divorce in '07, kicking off one of the longest and most expensive divorces in Illinois state history. There was no prenup, and DWade was responsible for paying both his and Siohvaughn's attorneys' fees, which totaled in the $10 million range.

That doesn't include the final $5 million settlement awarded to Siouvaughn in 2013. Siohvaughn and DWade are still dealing with custody issues. The court awarded DWade sole custody of their two sons in 2011, Siouvaughn accused him of orchestrating sole custody to avoid paying her more money in the divorce.

CHAPTER 12

Baby Mama's Golden Parachute

"Eighteen years, eighteen years. She got one of your kids,
got you for eighteen years."
—"Gold Digger" Kanye West

Have you looked around? Association is paying bills these days. Those lonely nights on the road, playing Russian roulette with different women, can lead to unexpected commitment. For some women, brokering their eggs for financial gain isn't a bad life plan. If they can't get a ring, they'll take the next best thing: eighteen years of child support.

The second verse of Kanye West's hit song "Gold Digger" accurately breaks down every professional athlete's fears when a woman pops up with an unplanned pregnancy. Visions of the mother spending money on everything but the child and funding a baller lifestyle with his cash. If the woman has started dating someone else, another ego trigger, with the assumption that another man will live off Mr. Professional Athlete's blood, sweat, and dollars.

Time Out:
This NFL star took his son's mother to court to have her child support reduced. Initially he was paying $200,000 a year. He wasn't late with his payments or trying to skip out on his responsibility, he just didn't want to pay for anything that wasn't directly going to his

child. The player was able to successfully get it lowered to $50,000 per year, because the judge ruled that the son's mother overstated her needs to the court and was in fact using the money to enhance her lifestyle. The mother had enrolled in college and was using some of the child support money for tuition. In addition to paying for a full-time nanny so she could attend school.

At the time, this NFL star was earning about $15 million per season. The child's mother argued that her son should be entitled to live in the same comforts as the two children he had with his wife. He dated both women at the same time; but chose his wife over his son's mother.

The son's mother referenced the sixteen-thousand-square-foot home he shared with his wife, the $5,000 per month cost of their personal chef, and the $16,000 he spent on one of his daughter's birthday parties as the reason she was entitled to the original order of support.

She also pointed out how the father was excluding her son from the same treatment as his half siblings. The NFL star and his family spent $40,000 per month or personal travel, with the children going on trips to New York, Atlanta, California, and Florida. Plus island and exotic destinations like Turks and Caicos, the Bahamas, Mexico, the Virgin Islands, and Rio de Janeiro.

The judge wasn't buying it. Although he did agree with the mother on one point. His other children attended private school and received health insurance benefits under their father's coverage. He ordered school tuition and health coverage added to the order of support.

Drama

Even if an athlete didn't have a brief affair or one-night stand, child support proceedings can still get pretty nasty. Ex-NBA star Gilbert Arenas and his reality TV star fiancée, Laura Govan, are a classic example of the battles that can turn former lovers into bitter enemies when lots of cash is at stake.

Let's rewind for a second. Gilbert and Laura met in 2002, while Gil played for the Warriors and Laura was coaching at a basketball camp affiliated with the team. They have four children together, but if you go by the information the two put out into the media, plus court documents, the relationship was volatile the entire time.

Back in 2008, Gilbert used to blog for NBA.com while he played for the Wizards. In addition to discussing all things basketball, Gilbert would detail areas of his personal life, including his relationship with Laura. He would often complain about her housekeeping, and even shared how frequently he kicked her out of the house.

Gil and Laura's first bitter child-support battle[13] happened in December 2005, following the birth of their oldest daughter, Izela. Gilbert and Laura have had at least four lawsuits against each other surrounding child support.

In 2011, one of the most infamous events took place during halftime of an NBA game. Laura had Gilbert served with child support documents as he was leaving the court for halftime of a game between the Magic and Miami Heat.

In the petition Laura wanted $109,000 in monthly support payments, or $1.3 million annually. She sued, claiming he abandoned her and their children. Laura reportedly even called the GM for the Magic at the time, Otis Smith, and told him, "If he doesn't abide by my demands, I will ruin this new start for him." In an interview, Gilbert gave an example of what he thought of Laura's claims by comparing her to a "bum on the street."[14]

---

13 http://www.washingtonpost.com/wp-dyn/content/article/2006/10/28/AR2006102800830.html

14 http://deadspin.com/5758824/gilbert-arenas-tells-you-all-about-his-conniving-baby-mama-and-dead-pet-sharks

That wasn't the first time Laura tried to have Gilbert served on the court. In 2005, she attempted to have him served while he was still with the Wizards, who were in Los Angeles to play the Lakers.

That time the Wizards caught wind of the plot and protected Gil by having him stay at the team hotel and claim to be sick for the game that night.

Gilbert fired his own warning shots; he filed suit against Laura and the producers of *Basketball Wives LA* to prevent Laura from speaking on him while on the show. The judge <u>dismissed the suit in 2012 because of comments Gil made on Twitter. The judge claimed Gil</u> couldn't claim privacy concerns when he was tweeting out thoughts and subject matter related to his suit. He and Govan reconciled soon after.

In 2015, the couple has once again broken up. Laura is suing Gilbert for child support, and for taking back her $1 million engagement ring. Laura once again claims he abandoned them. According to Gilbert, she receives $20,000 a month in child support.

It's not just black athletes that suffer from baby's mama drama. White athletes, even superstars, go through it, too:

NBA head coach Scott Skiles is on the list with six children, by an unknown number of women.

Former Boston Celtic great Larry Bird had baby mama drama while still in college at Indiana State.

Ex-Chicago Bear Brian Urlacher and former NFL quarterback Matt Leinart both had problems with their son's mothers. And, let's not forget, even the All-American pro Tom Brady had a bit of baby mama bad press. When Tom broke off a two-year relationship with actress

Bridget Moynahan and moved on to his current wife, Gisele, Moynahan discovered she was three months pregnant, and keeping her son.

Baby's Mama Golden Parachute

So what's considered fair? For an ex-girlfriend, child support can sometimes look like a "golden parachute." In business, that's a large payment or other form of financial compensation guaranteed to a company executive if they're fired unexpectedly. This is what is generally considered fair:

- A monthly cash sum starting at $10,000 per month minimum.
- A new home in either the city he plays in or the one he spends his off-season in, so he can be close to his kids, naturally. He pays the Mortgage of course. Not anything modest. Something bossy with a mortgage of at least $5,000 per month, of course adjusted based on location.
- All moving expenses paid for on his dime.
- A new car upgrade every 2.5 years.
- Private school, day care, medical insurance, and extracurricular activities paid for by the athlete.
- A life insurance policy that she and her child are the benefactors of.
- If said athlete is traded to a new team, then he has to reup on the house, car, and moving expense.

A top-tier parachute package could add up to over $100,000 per month. Imagine having to do that for multiple women.

Here's a little PSA: athletes are fed up with child support. It seemed to begin with Dwyane Wade and his divorce in 2008. He made the unconventional move of filing for full custody, despite the fact that he was a newly single professional athlete who travels extensively for his job.

We've seen an uptick in this trend with professional athletes over the last few years. Instead of paying $50,000 a month in child support, why not hire a nanny, plus the added assistance of friends and family to help raise the child? It's an idea that more professional athletes are exploring.

Here's a partial list of pro athletes that have sued for primary custody since 2010:

Dwight Howard

In 2007, the former Christian-athlete poster child, who once suggested the NBA logo should incorporate a cross, had a son with former Orlando Magic dancer turned reality TV star, Royce Reed. Dancers and players aren't supposed to mess around, but it happens. Having an out of wedlock child with an older woman, who also happened to be on the dance team didn't fit the image.

Reed sued Howard in April 2008 for child support—with a lot of the dirty details of their relationships and ensuing court battles playing out on Twitter.

By 2010, Dwight sued Royce for $9.2 million. $500 for every time she allegedly made remarks online that he termed "Dwight Bashing," according to court documents. He eventually won his suit, winning a judgment of $535,000 with a judge agreeing with Dwight that Royce violated the confidentiality agreement the two signed. He also was successful in having a gag order placed on her. Dwight and Royce have battled in court several times since then, and are currently locked in a custody battle for their son. During Royce's stint on *Basketball Wives Miami*, the court prevented her from mentioning Dwight's name or making any reference to him. In January 2015, Dwight began garnishing Royce's bank account to collect the judgment money. Dwight has six other children, from as many different women.

Chris Bosh

In a reoccurring theme, Chris Bosh is another athlete who sued his ex for custody, and to block her from airing their dirty laundry by appearing on *Basketball Wives Miami.*

According to his ex-girlfriend, Allison Mathis, Chris Bosh insisted that the two have a child before they got married. She claimed he took her to fertility treatments, but ended up breaking up with Mathis while she was pregnant, before eventually marrying his current wife, Adrienne.

Bosh was paying $2,600 a month in child support because he was ruled a resident of his home state of Texas, instead of Florida where he played with the Heat. That distinction prevented Mathis from filing for support in Florida where she was eligible to received $30,000 per month.

Paul George

In 2014, Pacers forward Paul George attempted to sue for custody of his daughter Olivia during a nasty child support battle with her mother, Daniela. George had a fling with the former stripper after they met in Miami following the Pacers loss in the playoffs. He reportedly offered Daniela $1,000,000 to abort the child. The two later agreed on a settlement with Daniela retaining physical custody of their daughter.

Deion Sanders

Football Hall of Famer and current NFL analyst Deion Sanders is another recent case. In 2014 Sanders filed a multimillion lawsuit against his ex-wife Pilar. Deion maintained that Pilar concocted a smear campaign against him that included publishing false statements on social media, accusing him of spousal abuse, child abuse, and assault[15]. Pilar lost custody of the couple's three children during a beastly divorce battle. Pilar even attempted to get the prenuptial agreement thrown out.

• • •

Whether it's fathers standing up for their rights, flipping the script on opportunist, or a calculated power move, it's a new day. Pushing out a child for a wealthy athlete does not guarantee a woman has hit the lottery and will become a millionaire by extension.

Even if she manages to score a big payday, the likelihood that she'll be able to live off that money for eighteen years is highly unlikely. Blowing money fast is a way of life for the pros.

---

15 http://jocksandstilettojill.com/2014/11/pilar-sanders-releases-audio-of-son-claiming-deion-sanders-is-abusive/

CHAPTER 13

Setups and Shakedowns

L ike Biggie said, "More money, more problems." The average athlete will likely become the target of someone looking to come up on Mr. Pro Athlete's kindness or stupidity. Whether it's a real estate investment, bad business advisors, or extortion, an athlete and their money will likely part.

Investment Schemes

In theory, an investment it's supposed to grow a jock's net worth. But in some cases, the athletes end up with more debt than profit. Somebody always knows a guy, that has a surefire way for the athlete to double up on his initial investment, risk free. These individuals could be family, close friends, business advisors, or even teammates.

Former NFL Hall of Famer Art Monk was a wide receiver with the Washington Redskins. Monk and a few other teammates decided to invest $50,000 each in a former teammate's shoe company. Ex-NFL tight end, Terry Orr's company turned out to be fake. There wasn't a shoe company. Orr used their seed money to pay off his debts. In 2001, he was sentenced to fourteen months in prison[16]

---

16 US News and World Reports.

First-round draft pick Fred Taylor invested his money with super agent William "Tank" Black. Tank represented many star athletes, including former NFL star Sterling Sharpe and NBA high flyer Vince Carter. He eventually accumulated over fifty professional athlete clients. Black was convicted for defrauding his clients via ponzi scheme, money laundering, and a Securities and Exchange Commission stock-swindling case. Taylor claims that Black's scheming cost him nearly his entire $5 million rookie signing bonus. Combined, Tank's former clients lost $12 million. He was sentenced to 51 months in federal prison.

Pussy Power

Another way athletes are setup: their love of quick and easy vagina. It's no secret that women are an easy way to shake jocks down. There are athletes who brought a girl home from the club, thinking they were headed for a happy ending, and woke up realizing they had been drugged and robbed. Some of these same guys were too ashamed to file a police report.

NFL defensive tackle Shaun Rogers had a similar experience. While Rogers was playing for the New York Giants in 2013, a woman he met during a night of partying in Miami robbed him.

Let me set the scene for you.

The life of a baller: you hit up Club Liv on a Sunday night. You're at your table, spitting up champagne, Hennessy, and vodka with the new lady friends you acquired, once they spotted the club sparklers and table overflowing with libations.

One of them gives you "the look," once she notices the way the spotlight makes the diamonds in your watch gleam and glisten. The party isn't over when the DJ stops spinning and the lights come on.

What's next? The hotel room of course. Rogers had a room at the Fontainebleau, where Club Liv is located. Naturally he invited the ladies up to the room to keep the party going.

That little adventure led to Rogers being robbed of a half million in jewelry and cash. Rogers said they returned to his hotel room around 7:00 a.m. He locked his valuables in the safe, and the party continued. Rogers fell asleep, and when he woke, the women plus his cash and jewels were gone.

Police later arrested a twenty-five-year-old woman[17] from Queens, NY. She and her friends were allegedly responsible for drugging and robbing several rich men in the Miami area.

Sometimes, even with an unfavorable HoFax, ballers still want to see what's up with it. Dating back to at least 2006, a "model" named Vanessa Lopez was accused by at least four professional athletes[18] of credit card theft, stalking, and extortion.

First up is former NBA player Delonte West:

Back in 2006, Delonte West was playing for the Boston Celtics. West ended up calling hotel security to have Lopez forced to leave his room in an Orlando hotel.

West claimed he had slept with Lopez in the past, she stopped by his hotel and wouldn't leave when he told her he was expecting company from another young lady. Vanessa had locked herself in the bathroom. When police arrived, Lopez countered and told them that West was mad because she wouldn't sleep with him on this particular night. She eventually left without further incident.

---

17 http://www.nfl.com/news/story/0ap1000000215583/article/woman-arrested-for-alleged-jewelry-robbery-of-shaun-rogers

18 http://www.nydailynews.com/entertainment/gossip/model-vanessa-lopez-linked-lineup-nba-stars-shaquille-o-neal-harassed-affair-article-1.462147

Next up, former number-one NBA draft pick Kenyon Martin. In 2007, Martin had a run in with Lopez while playing for the Denver Nuggets that ended with him filing charges against her.

In the report, Martin claimed that after a one-night stand, Lopez went into his wallet and took his credit card information without permission. She charged up $6485.90 worth of clothes while on-line shopping. Martin's bank notified him of the charges. The case was cracked when investigators checked the shipping address, which went to Lopez's address in Florida.

In 2010, Lopez filed a lawsuit against Shaq, claiming she was his mistress for five years—which would've covered the time she was dealing with Delonte and Kenyon. She claimed that once she broke up with Shaq, he began to harass and threaten her because she claimed she was pregnant and Shaq was married at the time. When she texted Shaq to tell him she was with child, he told her she should be sharing that information with whoever the father of the child was.

A Florida judge threw the case out of court, after catching Vanessa in several lies. Court documents from that case revealed another pregnancy hustle Vanessa allegedly tried to run.

In 2007 JJ Redick was a young second-year player with the Orlando Magic. Redick—or someone savvy in his life—was smart enough to put together a contract that stipulated that if Vanessa somehow became pregnant, he would pay her $25K to abort the pregnancy and go away quietly. The contract also called for her not to stalk or expose him as the potential father, should he decide the relationship was over.

In addition to that, the agreement required medical proof of an abortion, access to her medical records, and an exam by a doctor of his choice to verify any claims. That means he wanted to verify she was actually pregnant, and then make sure she really had the abortion.

There was also a gag order attached to the agreement to ensure that they didn't talk about it.

Extortion

Everyone has a past; sometimes the details in it aren't all that flattering. Recognizing how important image is to professional sports, unsavory characters won't hesitate to hold past transgressions over an athlete's head to extort some funds in exchange for their silence.

Usually a player will let his agent or lawyer know what's going on. The player's representatives then remind the extortionist that what is being proposed is a crime, and the extortionist goes away. And then there are times when the police are involved.

Coaches and announcers can get caught up with strippers and extortion plots, too. In this instance, we're looking at former Golden State Warriors coach and church pastor Mark Jackson. Jackson is a former NBA player who spent seventeen seasons in the L before moving into the broadcast booth and then coaching.

Jackson had a year-long affair in 2006 with a stripper named Alexis Adams. Jackson met the twenty-two-year-old Adams in New York while he was working as an analyst for the New Jersey Nets. Jackson sent Adams photos of his "naughty bits." She then shared the photos—plus a saved voice mail from Jackson— with Marcus Shaw. The ex-con hit Jackson up for $5,000 to fix his teeth and get his car out of impound...cause, goals...

Shaw approached Jackson in the lobby of a Memphis hotel with a folder of the photos. Jackson paid the initial $5,000. I guess Shaw thought about it and realized he could've gotten more money. He then sent the photos to Jackson's wife of twenty-two years, Desiree. The FBI got involved and set up a sting operation. Jackson offered Shaw and Adams $200,000 to make the situation go away. The FBI traced Shaw's IP address and cell phone info, and arrested the two on extortion charges. Among Shaw's previous charges were robbery, kidnapping, and murder.[19]

Ironically enough, in 1997 while Jackson was playing for the Indiana Pacers, strippers from Atlanta's Gold Club knocked on Jackson's hotel room door to offer their services. Jackson's response was, "No, thank you, I'm a married man. I'm very happily married."

---

19 http://www.thesmokinggun.com/documents/mark-jackson-extortion-plot-879234

CHAPTER 14

Sign Your Own Checks

Every athlete believes he's going to cash out. That the money will be there forever, and so will the opportunities to make more money. Michael Jordan is generally held up as the gold standard. Jordan along with Magic Johnson have given the blue print for what a successful post-career business life should look like. Shaquille O'Neal's contribution to this new, multifaceted brand athlete can't be forgotten either.

Before Shaq was drafted into the NBA in 1992, he already had several big-money endorsement deals. He was living the dream and went on to become a platinum-selling rapper, star in movies, and even score his own video game, *Shaq Fu*, all before he won an NBA title. When Shaq left the Orlando Magic in the summer of 1996 to join the Lakers, he literally forced the NBA to change the rules for free agency. The reason why restricted free agents exist in the NBA today is because the Magic lost Shaq to LA.

Shaq said one of the smartest things he did was invest in bonds early in his career. A safe investment that matures over time. He also bought several for his family. It was once reported that Shaq never spent an NBA paycheck; instead he lived off his endorsement deal money.

But Shaq was the exception and not the rule.

One NBA player shared with me the story about when he received his first NBA paycheck. He was completely blown away by the amount of money deducted in taxes. He literally called the bank to ask them what happened to the rest of his money. He had no idea that amount of money would be coming out each pay period.

Most athletes will likely encounter some financial issues. Even with the amount of information that's available. One of your favorite athletes will be on TV, begging some life coach or financial advisor to help them regain control of their life after blowing it all.

Your agent and/or your business manager should provide you with a monthly statement of every dollar spent. Including their charges for miscellaneous things like shipping, photo copies, your brother's monthly allowance, how much you blow in out-of-network ATM fees, etc. It's all there. The idea is to be informed on every part of the process involving *your* money. It's OK to ask questions. If you don't know how much money you're spending month to month, how will you plan for your future once your income drops? Or as your alimony and child support payments increase.

Families Sometimes Bankrupt You

Not all the families are just being greedy. I'm sure they mean well. Everybody has a business venture, idea, or plot. It makes perfect sense that Mr. Professional Athlete is expected to become a personal banker and road to their dreams.

But it's not just business ideas. There's a sob story around every corner. One person is about to lose their house, another a car, or has looming high medical bills. The problems are endless. Some are tricked out of their money. Pro athletes have unknowingly signed over power of attorney to family members. And others have had parents demand million-dollar paydays as a thank-you for the job of raising the athlete.

Then there are those who simply lived the high life, complete with all the pseudo trappings of superstar status.

In 2012 these were the amounts of an average yearly contract across the pro leagues:

NBA: $5.15 million

MLB: $3.2 million

NHL: $2.4 million

NFL: $1.9 million[20]

Time and time again we've heard how an opulent lifestyle of money, hoes, and clothes will blow up an athletes finances. When you ascribe to live a rock star lifestyle, you can't forget the maintenance attached to all that luxury.

These are my Top 5 Athlete Bankruptcy All-Stars:

NBA Champion Antoine Walker
Antoine Walker will always be on the list of bankruptcy all-stars for blowing through $110 million during a thirteen-year NBA career. That's not something Antoine or most people will forget quickly. The real estate market, gambling debts, and frivolous spending wiped out his fortune.

Ex-NFL Wide Receiver Terrell Owens
Former 1996 third-round NFL draft pick Terrell Owens spent fifteen seasons in the NFL with the Niners, Eagles, Cowboys, Bengals,

---

20 http://www.bloomberg.com/bw/magazine/content/11_06/b4214058615722.htm

and Bills. The $80 million or so he had made in his career is almost gone, but not because he tricked it off living a lavish lifestyle. Owens wasn't flashy or dripping in a lot of jewelry. He didn't pop a bunch of bottles, *but* he did have an area where he didn't practice restraint. T. O. lost his money through faulty representation, bad investments, and child support payments.

Owens said his financial advisers lured him into risky investments like an entertainment complex in his home state of Alabama that saw him lose $2 million. He also found out later that not only was the business illegal in the state, it also violated the NFL's policy of prohibiting players from investing in gambling businesses.

Then there was the "friend" who stole about $270,000 from Terrell.

His child support payments reached almost $50,000 a month for his four children, by four different women. Three of his four children's mothers sued for child support.

Terrell never seriously dated or was in relationships with his children's mothers, and also stated that he never intended to be seriously involved with the women. One was a one-night stand; the others were casual relationships. Three of the mothers appeared with Terrell on an episode of *Dr. Phil.*

For some reason, using a condom wasn't a part of the plan. Owens later said he was surprised that the women sued him, as he never thought they were the type. My question, would he really know if they were the "type," since he hardly knew them?

Former NFL Quarterback Vince Young
Vince Young was the third pick in the 2006 NFL draft by the Tennessee Titans. By thirty, Young was out of the NFL and filing

for Chapter 11 federal bankruptcy. Young's story is a virtual guide of how to lose millions as a pro athlete.

Vince's rookie deal with the Titans included $25.7 million in guaranteed money. During the 2011 NFL lockout, Young's financial advisor, Ronald Peoples, secured a $1.8 million loan that came with a 20 percent interest rate. By the time Young sued his financial advisor two years later in 2013, the interest had accumulated, and Young owed $2.5 million to Pro Player Funding.

Young sued Peoples, claiming he didn't authorize the loan. Peoples claimed in a deposition that Vince wanted to throw himself a birthday party that would cost $300,000. Peoples also said that though he tried to keep Vince on a monthly budget of around $30,000, Young's monthly expenses would sometimes run as high as $200,000. Some of the extravagances Young lavished on:

- $600 shots of Louis XIII from Morton's restaurants for his buddies.
- Splurging at TGI Friday's to the tune of $6000. Yes, you read that correctly, at TGI Friday's.
- One time Vince wanted to be alone on a Southwest Airlines flight, so he bought all the tickets.
- He reportedly had a Cheesecake Factory addiction, so he spent $5k a week there during his rookie season in Tennessee.

Young and Peoples eventually reached an out-of-court settlement.

In his six NFL seasons, Young spent time with the Titans, Eagles, and Bills—though never actually making it out of training camp with the latter—earning an estimated $34 million.

Boxing legend Mike Tyson

In the late eighties and early nineties, "Iron Mike" Tyson was the epitome of a sports superstar. Tyson won his first nineteen professional fights by knockout; very few opponents made it beyond round one.

According to the *New York Times*, Tyson earned $400 million in his boxing career, but filed for bankruptcy in 2003, with $27 million in debt. He also owed the IRS another $13 million in unpaid taxes, and $4 million to the British tax authorities.

Tyson's riches were spent on the usual: a $400,000 monthly maintenance for his lifestyle of mansions, jewelry, and luxury cars. He once threw himself a birthday party that cost him $400,000. Over a two-year period back in the nineties, Tyson spent $9 million on legal fees. He also developed an affinity for exotic pets like tigers, and an expensive drug habit.

He married three times, with his ex-wife Monica Turner receiving a $9 million divorce settlement. Tyson is the father of eight children.

Ex-NBA Star Kenny Anderson

Kenny Anderson earned an estimated $60 million during his NBA career after playing for nine different teams. The second pick of the 1991 NBA draft married three times. His divorce from his first wife, actress and reality TV star Tami Roman, was a killer. The two married in 1994, with Tami filing for divorce in 1998 and the divorce finally being granted in 2001. Although there was a prenup, Roman successfully challenged it and was awarded half his assets at the time, and $8,500 a month in child support.

To celebrate her court victory, she had a custom license plate made for a Hummer that read "HISCASH." However, by 2005 Kenny had filed for bankruptcy and stopped making his child support payments. At one point, Tami and her two daughters had to receive public assistance. Tami sued Kenny for the back child support, with the two finally settling for $800,000 in 2012. Kenny will be making those payments from his NBA pension in monthly installments.

Anderson fathered seven children by five women. His oldest daughter is with Dee Dee Roper, better known as Spinderella from the eighties rap group Salt N Pepa.

During the NBA lockout in 1998, Kenny detailed his spending habits in an interview. At that time, Anderson was making $5.8 million a year. He owned eight cars, an estate in Beverly Hills, and had a monthly allowance of $10,000 that he called his "hanging out money." His expenses included[21]:

- $75,000 a year on car insurance and maintenance for those eight cars mentioned, which included a Porsche Carrera, customized Range Rover, a Lexus, and a Mercedes.
- $250,000 a year on a vanity marketing company named Kenny the Kid Enterprises. The company managed Tami and employed five friends.
- $175,000 annually on lawyers and accountants' fees.
- $7,200 per month in child support.
- $42,000 a year for Tami's spending allowance.

At the time of his bankruptcy filing, he had $41,000 in monthly expenses to pay, with an annual income of $150,000.

Oprah Winfrey gave Serena Williams this financial advice, "always sign your own checks." By doing so, it gives you accountability for the money being spent.

Both the NFL and NBA offer programs to help players learn about managing their money more effectively.

---

21 http://www.nytimes.com/1998/10/26/sports/pro-basketball-when-millionaires-are-laid-off.html

CHAPTER 15

Exit Strategy

Nobody wants to think about the end. When you are twenty-five, have loads of cash, women, and access to all the best life has to offer, it's sort of hard to think long term. As talented as an athlete is, to quote the great Charles Barkley, "Father time is undefeated." It's why the athletes play second to the owners on the business side of things. Your body will breakdown. Deep-pocketed owners aren't relying on their strength or quickness to get their job done. They can still be the man with a balky knee at fifty.

A big problem for athletes is the lack of a transition plan. They've been so focused on being the best that they never put any thought into what they'll do once they're done playing. Very few will be able to shut it down on their own terms. A winner never wants to put thought into the next game before they finish the one they're in, but a great plan will make it easier to sail off into the sunset.

Must Be the Money

The NFL and the NBA have programs to aid in the transition from professional athlete to regular Joe. Most players either don't know it's available or fail to make use of it. It's usually their wives who investigate these areas for them. We've all heard the statistics: 78 percent of NFL players go broke three years after retirement, and 60 percent of NBA players go broke within five years of stepping off the court. Let's say you didn't do so great with managing your money. All isn't lost.

The NBA offers one of the most generous pension plans[22] for its athletes. The athletes contribute 5 percent to 10 percent of their salary. Players are fully vested after playing in the league for just three years. They can begin to draw their pension at fifty. The annual benefit, for a guy with the three-year minimum, would be $19,160.

If the guy has a lengthy career, let's say he played in the league for ten years, the payment rises to $60,000 annually. If he can wait until age sixty-two, those that meet the three-year minimum, their payment would jump to $60,000 annually from the $19,160. For those with ten or more years, the payment would be $200,000 annually.

NFL players also become vested in their pension after three seasons. The benefits are calculated using credits earned for each season played. For example, a player who spends five years in the NFL, and decides to draw his pension at fifty-five, will receive an annual payment of $28,200.

The MLB retirement plan is similar to the NBA's, except that players aren't fully vested until after ten seasons. If the player starts drawing his pension at sixty-two, his annual payments will be about $200,000 per year.

Shoe Money and Endorsements

Michael Jordan is the platinum standard. The first NBA billionaire, Jordan signed his original five-year deal with Nike in 1984 for $500,000 annually, plus royalties. By 2015, those earnings are estimated at $100 million[23]. Jordan earned $92 million from his NBA contracts during his career.

---

22 http://www.investopedia.com/financial-edge/0710/top-pro-athlete-pension-plans.aspx

23 http://www.businessinsider.com/michael-jordan-nike-deal-believed-to-be-

We know there's only one Mike. The average athlete will not see more money from their endorsement deals once they retire. Some won't even maintain those relationships throughout their playing days.

According to the 2013 list of the "one hundred highest-paid athlete endorsement[24] deals," twenty-six are held by MLB players, eighteen of those on the list are NBA players, and the NFL has fifteen. This list contains 70 percent of the money brands spend on endorsements. The lowest-paid player to make the top one hundred list was Dodger Carl Crawford with $75,000 that year. The odds aren't in your favor.

The reality is, few athletes are getting major endorsement money. And realistically, the money isn't always what the average person envisions. Let's say for example a midlevel basketball player signs a deal with Nike. That deal might be for only $150,000. Of that $150,000, $20,000 might be for product—shoes, tracksuits, limited releases, etc. Oh, you thought there was an endless supply of free shoes? Nope. That leaves $130,000 cash, and while that's a lot of money to the average person, that's less than 10 percent of the average pro athlete's salary. Add to that the demand for a retired athlete's services drops dramatically, so any money earned would likely be event based, and not assured future income.

Top 5 Postcareer Choices for Athletes and Why They Better Have a Plan B:
Playing overseas or in Canada

You could continue to play. For the football player who still has the desire to play, your best options are the Canadian Football League. Rookies start out at around $50,000. If you opt for the arena league route, pay is about $400 per game, or $7,200 for an eighteen-game

100-million-a-year-2015-3

24 http://opendorse.com/blog/top-100-highest-paid-athlete-endorsers-of-2013/

season. By comparison, a practice squad spot in the NFL will get you $6,000 per week.

Still trying to live out your hoop dreams? You can play in the NBA's D-League while your agent works on a call-up. Life in the D-League is very different from life in the NBA. Average crowd size is about twenty-five hundred. College games pull larger crowds. No private charter flights and no five-star hotel accommodations. D-League salary is between $13,000 and $25,000 a season[25]. If a player is lucky to be called up to the big leagues, their minimum salary will jump to $507,336 for the 2014–15 season.

Or you can head overseas. The money is more, but you're far away from home, and it can get lonely. Many teams provide accommodations for players, including an apartment and a car. But that doesn't mean the apartment isn't a bit sketchy.

Depending on the level of the league, the travel is less hectic than the D-League as most teams play fewer games over a longer period of time. Each country has its own league, but unlike the NBA, there's no player's union to protect players from shady situations that arise. Having the right mindset is key because it's a huge cultural adjustment.

Ask NBA star JR Smith. JR went to China for a portion of the 2011 NBA lockout season. Clashes with coaches, and a brawl in the stands between his family and Chinese fans, made for an uneasy existence. JR's team fined him $1 million for being late and missing practices. That was one-third of his salary.

Former NBA All-Star Stephon Marbury headed to China after his time in the NBA and won three CBA (Chinese Basketball Association) championships in four years; he even has a bronze statue there.

---

25 RidiculousUpside.com

The average overseas player can make a starting salary between $65,000 and $100,000 per season, often untaxed.

Coaching

Maybe you want to be a coach? Most aren't going to walk off the court and be like Jason Kidd. Kidd retired from the New York Knicks after being bounced from the playoffs in the 2013 season. He was hired as the Brooklyn Nets' head coach in June. Kidd had led the Nets to the NBA Finals, twice in '02 and '03. He jumped ship, after the end of a rocky season, for the Milwaukee Bucks. Sounds hot, right? But then, there are cases like NBA legend Patrick Ewing.

The former Knicks legend hasn't been able to get a head coaching job in the NBA, even though he's been an assistant coach for the last decade. Ewing has been an assistant with the Washington Wizards, Houston Rockets, Orlando Magic, and Charlotte Hornets. Despite a fifteen-year NBA career, where he was voted as one of the top fifty NBA players, and first ballot Hall of Famer, Ewing hasn't had a shot in the hot seat.

The average NBA and NFL coaches' salaries mirror each other at a little less than $4 million per year. However, the NFL has more big-name coaches making major figures at over $6 million per season. Of NBA head coaches, Doc Rivers sits comfortably on top. The former NBA guard, and current head coach and team president of the Clippers, is estimated to earn $10 million per year.

Let's say you're a bit more realistic. You're cool with taking an assistant coach position. On the high end, NBA assistants make about $1 million per season, while NFL assistants come in around $1.3 million.

But those are the highs; the average NBA assistant coach earns about $50,000 per year[26]. That includes the new titles like player development coaches. Most of those guys are former players trying to work their way up the ranks. It's a win-win because it's a bridge to the younger players often times, and a way to get used to the game from the other end of the bench. The D-League is also an entry for guys wanting to coach. The salary of a winning D-League head coach is about $100K.

The former players who have the best shot at securing a head coach or assistant role so soon after their playing days have ended will be the ones who can quickly make adjustments to the corporate aspect of sports. You can't continue with the same behavior you indulged in during your playing days.

Especially as an assistant coach. If you crave the limelight, this isn't the best career path to choose. In addition to the money, there's something else that will change. It's not a good look for coaches to go out partying and drinking with the athletes. It's the coaches and the players. Co-mingling is frowned upon.

Relationships matter. The connections you make while playing will be your best ally. Plus, this keeps you close to the game, even if your body isn't cooperating.

Perhaps you can take the owner-investor approach. Shadow some of Jay Z's moves by moving from ownership to agency. Try and buy into a team like Magic Johnson did with the Lakers, or Shaquille O'Neal with the Sacramento Kings.

On-Air Analyst
ESPN, Fox Sports, NFL Network, MLB channel, NBA TV, *Inside the NBA*, plus a host of regional and college networks, that sounds

---

26 http://www.cbssports.com/nba/writer/ken-berger/24723463/for-many-nba-assistants-the-road-to-glory-is-well-traveled

like plenty of space for former athletes to take to the airwaves and work after the final whistle.

The reality, there are only so many roles out there. And not every athlete is charismatic enough to become a media darling. Both the NFLPA (National Football League Players Association) and NBPA (National Basketball Players Association) offer sports journalism boot camps where athletes can learn the ropes from the pros of broadcast journalism, plus start forming those important connections with network producers and talent bookers that they're going to be turning to for work once the final buzzer sounds.

Remember my athlete breakdown from Chapter 1? Let's apply it here. Superstars can earn between $1 million to $2 million a year. Stars, between $200,000 to $400,000. Midlevel role players, they take home between $50,000 to $100,000 annually.[27] If an athlete requires training, that will be taken off the top of their salary, too.

So coaching and commentating didn't make the cut. Here are some other areas where pro athletes have found success in their postplaying days:

Hollywood: Entertainment and New Media

"I swear sports and music are so synonymous 'cause we want to be them, and they want to be us."—Drake

Sports and entertainment are in a long-term relationship at this point. Both have borrowed elements from each other to expand their business models. The NBA, NFL, and MLB have all been involved in the production of reality TV through shows like HBO's

---

27 http://www.hollywoodreporter.com/news/ray-lewis-shannon-sharpe-business-604890

Hard Knocks, which focuses on NFL training camp, or NBA TV's *Real Training Camp* series.

We're all familiar with the number of athletes that have tried their hand at rapping. Shaq is a platinum-selling rapper, Allen Iverson's mixtape was killed because it was too edgy for the times, Kobe... sigh. We just won't speak on that.

Most recently Kevin Durant expressed interest, while Stephen Jackson and Iman Shumpert have both put out mixtapes. But this isn't the nineties; music artists are barely making money from the sale of their music.

Maybe you want to act. Become the next Rick Foxx. The three-time NBA champ and ex-husband of singer-actress Vanessa L. Williams has forty-one film and TV credits to his name, including roles in sports-themed projects like *He Got Game, Eddie, The Game, Hit the Floor, Arliss, and Blue Chips*. Foxx also still works as an NBA analyst.

Ok, in front of the camera isn't for you. Perhaps you want to try film producing. Former NBA players Michael Finely, Baron Davis, and Jalen Rose are just some of the names that have produced projects for film, TV, and the web.

Franchises

Throw a jersey on the wall, name a chicken special after your sweet move, and you have all the makings for an entry into the booming business of franchise. That's what they'll sell you anyway. While there are definitely some athletes that are cleaning up, franchises fail with alarming frequency. Be committed and understand the financials.

Former Milwaukee Bucks player Junior Bridgeman is one of the success stories. He owns nearly 300 restaurants (including 162

Wendy's and 121 Chili's). Bridgeman's peak salary while playing with the Clippers in the mid-eighties was $350,000. During the off-seasons, Bridgeman learned the Wendy's franchise business in and out, by working in a local Wendy's. By the end of his NBA career, Bridgeman owned three Wendy's. Recently he went into partnership with retired NBA champion Chauncey Billups for thirty Wendy's.

Magic Johnson has had a lot of success with franchise operations. Magic has owned several franchise operations including Starbucks, Magic Johnson Theaters, TGI Fridays, 24 Hour Fitness, and Fat Burger.

• • •

Ok, you want to be a rebel? Here are a few other areas that are on the hot and bubbling list for postcareer options for retired athletes:

Fashion

Former Giants RB Carl Banks made the leap into fashion. Banks said he began his fashion career his second year in the league. Twenty years later, he parlayed that experience into reigniting the classic Starter brand, plus having license across all the sports leagues, including college, on items ranging from T-shirts to outerwear to ladies' apparel.

If an Instagram vixen can do it, why not a pro athlete?

Tech and Venture Capitalism

NBA players Andre Iguodala, Carmelo Anthony, and Amare Stoudemire are all dabbling in this area while still playing in the league. Anthony's M7 Tech Partners focused on the areas of wearable technology, while Chris Bosh announced plans to jump into the Miami area start up tech scene.

Motivational Speaker

Everybody else is doing it, right? You made it to the professional level. That's inspiring. I'm sure you've overcome a few things in life. Do you have a ring? Win again! Pimp your ring to score more speaking engagements. People always want to hear from a winner.

My final pieces of advice:

Health

Eat right and take care of your body. With the advancements in technology, athletes are currently faster and stronger. It's absolutely possible to extend your playing days through nutrition and alternative activities like yoga. One of the most frequent regrets you hear from older players and ex-athletes is the wish that they took better care of their bodies when they were younger.

Being a player costs. If your hobby is women, expect it to be an expensive one:

- Use discretion.
- Wrap up. You wouldn't leave a million dollars lying around just anyone. That's how jocks should think about their sperm. You can't just deposit it anywhere. You have to be your own hero, and protect yourself.
- Don't get married before you're done playing the field. Divorce is expensive. Prenup or not. It's cheaper to keep her. But peace of mind beats both those choices.

Life after playing professionally can be rough. Some of the noted issues that plague athletes following retirement:

- Many will go through depression once they are no longer in the spotlight. Life is different, you've been used to a schedule that has you traveling for games for months at a time. Then training to get ready for the season. Missing the camaraderie with teammates and the thrill of being able to play in front of twenty thousand people every night.

- Health issues.
- We've already mentioned the financial impact expected, and the likelihood of divorce. Both the athlete and his wife will have to make adjustments. Retirement means day in and day out together. Sometimes they discover they don't know each other anymore, or simply don't like each other.

That's why it's crucial to have a plan for what comes next once your playing days are over.

CONCLUSION

Life Comes at You Fast

The Internet has shown fans that outside their game day heroics, not every pro is a nice guy whose innermost thoughts you want to be exposed to.

As fans, we have to realize that athletes are people. Not all of them are passionate about the game. Some look at it as just a job that gets them a very large paycheck. Just like there are days you show up at work feeling like Marshawn Lynch's Super Bowl media day reply, "I'm just here so I won't get fined," they experience it, too.

Sometimes at the end of the season, all they want is for it to end, so they can start fresh next year: One...two...three...Cancun[28].

Not every athlete is cut out to be a role model. Can you still cheer for him or his team despite that knowledge?

For the athletes, if the plan is to profit off a branded identity, one where fans buy into your lifestyle and put their hard-earned funds down to support your efforts, you have to get comfortable with critiques. As a "brand," consumers are your number-one priority. Whether it's the media, Twitter trolls, or fans of the game. People

---

28 Reference to Nick Van Exel in Lakers huddle before Lakers got knocked out of Utah playoff series

will have opinions and unsolicited feedback. Part of your job is to take those darts with grace.

It takes the average athlete three to four seasons to develop as a pro, finding a successful balance between the game, the lifestyle, and the business side of sports. The irony in that is, that it matches the average length of most pro athletes' careers.

That's why it's crucial not to get too caught up and lose sight of the goal. Being a superstar comes with more money and fame, but also added expectations. You know that old saying, to whom much is given, much is required.

The clock is ticking.

GLOSSARY

Birdcall: Commonly used on social media to announce a city or location an athlete is in. Example, "What up, LA?"

Boom boom room: Player's room on the road where spare condoms, erroneous women, and general fun go down in.

Catfish: Taken from the documentary and MTV show. A "catfish" is a person who pretends to be someone else online (looks, personality, etc.).

Cheat ring: A ring given after a guy has a major mess-up.

Dial and deliver: Using social media for quick and easy sex.

Friend of the hoes: A male or female who is useful to girls because they know all the jocks. And to the jocks because they always know all the "bad chicks."

Helmet head syndrome: NFL players looking for attention because they aren't as high profile as other professional athletes.

HoFax: Details of a person's sexual history shared as a warning or endorsement.

Kardashian effect: The desire to gain reality TV fame. Exploiting personal relationships for popularity and social relevance.

New millennial athlete: The generation of professional athletes born between 1983–95 impacted by global branding, hip-hop, and the Internet.

Painkiller: A gift or bauble given after an embarrassing or public scandal in a relationship.

Post-Game Pass: A section of the stadium or arena designated for players to connect with friends and family for a few minutes after the game.

Professional friend: A friend of a professional athlete whose job it is to be a part of the entourage.

Ring Protection: preferential treatment because an athlete won a championship

Roadkill: Groupies who hook up with athletes while they're on road trips.

Slash: A person who lists multiple jobs as their occupation. They model, do hair, and work in PR. Their city is listed New York/Miami/LA/Houston with little plane icons.

Star panties: Instagram models, Twitter honeys, also known as Thots. Girls on social media with "for booking info" in the bio.

The life: The lifestyle away from the game, associated with professional athletes. All the perks of celebrity.

The help: Same as "professional friend."

The work: Groupies and side chicks. Jocks refer to the random girls they have sexual relations with.

Thots: "That ho over there."

Turn up: The ultimate party state. High-key fun. Can also include drugs and alcohol.

Acknowledgments

Sending a million thank-yous and love to all the individuals who encouraged me to write this, allowed me to interview them or gave vital input. You are appreciated:

Ronni, Mommy, Andrea Kelly, Tosha Lewis, Kesha Myers, Shawn Harrison, Kellie Williams, Des Brown, Drew Greer, Sunni Watson, Channon Thompson, Nikki Thagard, Marissa Mosley, Tamula Walker, Mark Jarrell, Robert Littal - BSO, Freshalina, DerMarr Johnson, Chad Johnson, Cari Champion, Robyn Young, Illinois State Sen. Napoleon Harris, Tamara Gregory, Mimi Blanchard, LaTanya Newt, Tiffany Mills, Robert Ector, Syreeta Hubbard- The NFL Chick, Udochi, Megan Inaba, Clone, and YOU.

Author's Page

Jill Munroe is the creator of the sports and pop culture site, *Jocks and Stiletto Jill*. The site's mantra is "ESPN meets Sex and the City." Jill provides visitors with an insider's playbook to connect the dots between off-the-field shenanigans and in-game excellence.

The Los Angeles-based sports culture analyst was named by Ebony.com as one of the top black women sports bloggers; has been featured on sites like FoxSports.com and Complex, and is also a frequent guest on ESPN radio, Yahoo Sports 730, and NPR. Munroe has worked on projects with some of the biggest names in sports and entertainment, while employed at corporate powerhouses like; Nike, Sony Pictures Entertainment, BET Networks, and Virgin Records. As a fan, Jill is in a complicated relationship with both the Lakers and Clippers. She cites the NBA as her first love, and the NFL is her sidepiece.

Stay Connected with Jill Munroe

JocksandStilettoJill.com

Email: Info@JocksandStilettoJill.com

Twitter: @StilettoJill

Facebook: Facebook.com/JocksandStilettoJill

Instagram: @StilettoJill

YouTube: YouTube.com/StilettoJill

BIBLIOGRAPHY

West, Kanye. "Gold Digger." 2005

Ross, Rick. "Stay Scheming." 2012

Twista, featuring Kanye West. "Overnight Celebrity" 2004

Jay Z. "Excuse Me, Miss."

Steve Francis quote – January 2005 http://sports.espn.go.com/nba/news/story?id=1964511

Eric Williams 2011.

Kool Moe Dee "They Want Money" 1989.

Drake. "Thank Me Now." 2010

Drake. "6 Man." 2015

Too Short, Jay Z. "Blow the Whistle remix." 2008

Lil Wayne. "Pop Bottles."

Notorious BIG "Mo Money, Mo Problems" 1997

Herm Edwards 2011 NFL Rookie Symposium.

Barbara Walters interview with Mike Tyson. *20/20*. ABC Network. 1988.

Pete Holmes' podcast, "You made it weird" March 2014

O'Neal, Shaquille. *Uncut*. New York: Grand Central Publishing, 2011

Tyson, Mike. *Undisputed Truth*. Blue Rider Press, 2013.

Bush, Jacklyn. *The Gold Club*. Los Angeles, Ca: Milligan Books, 2003.

Bailey, Troy. "*Love Don't Cost a Thing*." Warner Bros. 2003.

Williams, Mo. Twitter comments July 2010. Twitter.com.

Allen, Ray. Twitter comments. December 2009. Twitter.com.

Crites, Todd, Jackson Nguyen. *30 Days in May*. Showtime. 2013.

Chopra, Gotham. *Kobe Bryant's Muse*. Showtime. 2015

ESPN the Magazine. November 2014.

Sandomir, Richard. "Tyson's Bankruptcy Is a Lesson In Ways to Squander a Fortune." *New York Times*. August 2013.

"The average NBA Player will make a lot more than other sports." Business Insider. http://www.businessinsider.com/chart-the-average-nba-player-will-make-lot-more-in-his-career-than-the-other-major-sports-2013-10

http://bleacherreport.com/articles/2365532-kevin-durant-comments-on-relationship-with-media-at-2015-nba-all-star-weekend?utm_source=twitter.com&utm_medium=referral&utm_campaign=programming-national

http://www.essence.com/2011/08/15/real-talk-are-you-giving-up-on-black-love/

Erving, Julius Dr. J: The Autobiography, Harper Luxe 2013

Shaunie O'Neal's comments in a 2010 *Essence* interview regarding her divorce from Shaq

http://nypost.com/2013/11/24/the-night-tiger-woods-was-exposed-as-a-serial-cheater/

http://www.nydailynews.com/entertainment/gossip/erin-barry-tony-parker-sexting-relationship-physical-reports-article-1.452204

http://www.ibtimes.com/derek-jeter-girlfriends-who-has-yankees-star-dated-photos-1555422

http://abcnews.go.com/blogs/entertainment/2012/12/mike-tyson-on-catching-brad-pitt-with-his-ex-robin-givens/

http://www.people.com/people/archive/article/0,,20136227,00.html

http://www.nytimes.com/2009/08/09/sports/football/09marriage.html

http://www.washingtonpost.com/wp-dyn/content/article/2006/10/28/AR2006102800830.html

http://deadspin.com/5758824/gilbert-arenas-tells-you-all-about-his-conniving-baby-mama-and-dead-pet-sharks

http://jocksandstilettojill.com/2014/11/pilar-sanders-releases-audio-of-son-claiming-deion-sanders-is-abusive/

US News and World Reports.

http://www.nfl.com/news/story/0ap1000000215583/article/woman-arrested-for-alleged-jewelry-robbery-of-shaun-rogers

http://www.nydailynews.com/entertainment/gossip/model-vanessa-lopez-linked-lineup-nba-stars-shaquille-o-neal-harassed-affair-article-1.462147

http://www.thesmokinggun.com/documents/mark-jackson-extortion-plot-879234

http://www.bloomberg.com/bw/magazine/content/11_06/b4214058615722.htm

http://www.nytimes.com/1998/10/26/sports/pro-basketball-when-millionaires-are-laid-off.html

http://www.investopedia.com/financial-edge/0710/top-pro-athlete-pension-plans.aspx

http://www.businessinsider.com/michael-jordan-nike-deal-believed-to-be-100-million-a-year-2015-3

http://opendorse.com/blog/top-100-highest-paid-athlete-endorsers-of-2013/

RidiculousUpside.com

http://www.cbssports.com/nba/writer/ken-berger/24723463/for-many-nba-assistants-the-road-to-glory-is-well-traveled

http://www.hollywoodreporter.com/news/ray-lewis-shannon-sharpe-business-604890

www.ingramcontent.com/pod-product-compliance
Lightning Source LLC
Chambersburg PA
CBHW031849090426
42741CB00005B/412